"*At the Feet of Ordinary Women* is a refreshing 'how-to' guide for women longing to live Titus 2:4-5 in the real world! The authors' wonderfully honest dialogue and thought-provoking questions will gently guide your heart to the One who knows the hearts of women like none other. Savor each lesson and move at your own pace as these wonderful ladies share their victories and struggles as wives, mothers, and lovers of Jesus Christ!"

—Julie Barnhill, speaker; author of
She's Gonna Blow! Real Help for Moms Dealing with Anger

"This is a wonderful book packed with practical advice for ordinary women who simply want to be all they can be for God. Who better to write such a book than five ordinary women whose lives demonstrate that God adds his extraordinary touch to the lives of those who make it their regular practice to sit at His feet? And I ought to know — I'm their pastor!"

—Calvin Rychener, pastor, Northwoods Community Church

D1358164

AT THE FEET OF
Ordinary ~~WISE~~
WOMEN

Finding Your Self in Titus 2:4-5

ANGIE CONRAD, JANET COX, TAMMY EAGAN,

SANDY KERSHAW, AND PAM MILLER

NAVPRESS

Bringing Truth to Life
P.O. Box 35001, Colorado Springs, Colorado 80935

OUR GUARANTEE TO YOU

We believe so strongly in the message of our books that we are making this quality guarantee to you. If for any reason you are disappointed with the content of this book, return the title page to us with your name and address and we will refund to you the list price of the book. To help us serve you better, please briefly describe why you were disappointed. Mail your refund request to: NavPress, P.O. Box 35002, Colorado Springs, CO 80935.

The Navigators is an international Christian organization. Our mission is to reach, disciple, and equip people to know Christ and to make Him known through successive generations. We envision multitudes of diverse people in the United States and every other nation who have a passionate love for Christ, live a lifestyle of sharing Christ's love, and multiply spiritual laborers among those without Christ.

NavPress is the publishing ministry of The Navigators. NavPress publications help believers learn biblical truth and apply what they learn to their lives and ministries. Our mission is to stimulate spiritual formation among our readers.

© 2002 by Angie Conrad, Janet Cox, Tammy Eagan, Sandy Kershaw, and Pam Miller

ISBN 1-57683-301-1

Cover design by Dan Jamison
Cover illustration by Greg Hargreaves/Artville
Creative Team: Nanci McAlister, Keith Wall, Pat Miller

Some of the anecdotal illustrations in this book are true to life and are included with the permission of the persons involved. All other illustrations are composites of real situations, and any resemblance to people living or dead is coincidental.

Unless otherwise identified, all Scripture quotations in this publication are taken from the HOLY BIBLE: NEW INTERNATIONAL VERSION® (NIV®). Copyright © 1973, 1978, 1984 by International Bible Society. Used by permission of Zondervan Publishing House. All rights reserved. Other versions used include: the *New American Standard Bible* (NASB), © The Lockman Foundation 1960, 1962, 1963, 1968, 1971, 1972, 1973, 1975, 1977; *The Message: New Testament with Psalms and Proverbs* (MSG) by Eugene H. Peterson, copyright © 1993, 1994, 1995, used by permission of NavPress Publishing Group; the *New King James Version* (NKJV). Copyright © 1982 by Thomas Nelson, Inc. Used by permission. All rights reserved.

At the feet of ordinary women / Angie Conrad ... [et al.].
    p. cm.
Includes bibliographical references.
  ISBN 1-57683-301-1
  1. Women--Religious life. I. Conrad, Angie, 1956-
BV4527 .A88 2002
248.8'43--dc21
                                        2002006625

Printed in the United States of America

1 2 3 4 5 6 7 8 9 10 / 06 05 04 03 02

FOR A FREE CATALOG OF
NAVPRESS BOOKS & BIBLE STUDIES,
CALL 1-800-366-7788 (USA)
OR 1-416-499-4615 (CANADA)

To my mentors: Delores, Phyllis, Bev, Lois, and Audrey. I am forever grateful for your experience, love, and dedication in wanting me to be the person God intended. Thank you.

To my mom and dad, who didn't live to read this. I know you are proud of me and are cheering me on from heaven.

To my stepdad, Dan. You always believed in me. And I am thankful God brought you into my life.

—ANGIE

To the women in my family, young and old, who were and are a part of who I am today: Grandma Sarah; Grandma Bessie; my mom; and my only daughter, Angela, who this year gave me two of the greatest joys in my life—twin granddaughters, Katherine Anne and Lucy Grace.

—JANET

To my grandmothers, who are my examples in persevering through trials, working hard, and loving their families through it all. To my mother, Jan, who continues to pour out her love to me. And to my daughter, Valerie— may your life shine with the best in us all.

—TAMMY

*To my daughter, Kristin, and daughter-in-law Mandy,
beautiful young women who are learning to live out
Titus 2:4-5 in their lives.*
—SANDY

᠅ ◇ ᠅

*To those who desire to be more like Jesus and share His
good news with others. May God continue to work in
and through you, "both to will and to work for His
good pleasure" (Philippians 2:13, NASB).*
—PAM

CONTENTS

ACKNOWLEDGMENTS

FROM ANGIE:
Thank you, Bruce, Andy, and Sam for giving me great stories to write about! I love you.

Thanks to my friends at Northwoods Community Church for your prayers and encouragement.

Thank you, Tammy, for being bold in listening to God's idea for this project.

Thanks to my Care Group—your love sustains me.

Jennie Dimkoff, thanks for giving me the NavPress connection.

Julie Barnhill, thank you so much for your tips and cheerleading!

Janet Kenton, you gave me my first encouragement to write. Thanks for telling me you liked my "style."

Laura, you are my best friend and prayer partner for life. Thanks for our many great years together.

Sandy, thanks for keeping me sane!

FROM SANDY:
Thank you to my husband, Steve, who has always believed in me. Without you, I would have nothing to write! I love you.

Thanks to my son, Jeff. Your prayers, encouraging notes, and love motivated me to press on.

My sister Karen, my prayer warrior, thank you for caring and seeing the need for this material.

Thanks to Angie for spearheading this project and formatting all the material I sent you.

FROM JANET:

Thank you to my guys, who are always an encouragement: Allen, my husband of thirty-five years; and my three sons, Joel (thanks, Joel, for your lovely wife, Helen), Christopher, and Kerry James. Thanks for being there!

Thanks to Mary Lou Birdsall and the women of First United Brethren Church, Peoria, Illinois, for the mentoring you gave to me by your Christlike examples. I now pass that along.

Thanks to my special friends who prayed often for me during the writing of this book: Joan, Paula, Lois, Sandy, Carole, and Carolyn.

FROM TAMMY:

Thank you to the men in my life: my husband, Tom, who sees all my failures but focuses on my strengths and never let's me give up on God's call; my sons, Kevin and Eric, for putting up with a mom who is often distracted and forgetful; my dad, Larry, who told me that I can do anything I set my mind to; and my friend Tony Myrick, who taught and modeled a "theology of friendship."

Thank you to the "dream team" of authors who worked together on this book. Especially Angie Conrad, who envisioned sharing this message with women beyond our local church and had the courage to walk through opened doors.

Thank you also to the staff and people of St. George's Church in Stamford, England. You have confirmed God's call in my life in a powerful way. Thank you for allowing me into your lives for this little while; you'll live in my heart forever.

FROM PAM:

Thanks to the many women who cared enough to invest their lives in me and who lived out 1 Thessalonians 2:8.

Thanks to Bill and Sue Tell, Jim Rinella, Janet Dunn, and Becky Brodin. You were great sources of encouragement to me while I was on staff with The Navigators. Thank you for the many hours you invested in me and for the leadership and ministry skills you taught me. I appreciate you!

Thanks to Sandy for teaching me so much about writing and for all your encouragement. You are, indeed, an inspiration and example to me.

Thanks to my "moms' group," especially Becky, Lisa, and Dalona. I treasure each of your friendships. Thanks for the growth you have brought in my life as a result of knowing you.

Thanks to my husband, Kevin, and children, Brandon and Amber, for your patience with this book project. Even though it took many hours of my time away from you, you knew the possible impact of this book and for that, you were supportive. Thank you, family! I love you!

Then [the older women] can train the younger women to love their husbands and children, to be self-controlled and pure, to be busy at home, to be kind, and to be subject to their husbands, so that no one will malign the word of God.

Titus 2:4-5

God Never Intended You to Fly Solo

By Angie Conrad

R elationships . . . who needs them?

By design, we all do.

But why are relationships often so difficult? Shouldn't they be easier? Since God invented them, how could something so right go so wrong?

God created man in order to have fellowship with Him. He then created woman to have relationship with man. It's not good to be alone, He told Adam. Indeed, God intended each of us to benefit from the support and encouragement of family, friends, neighbors, and fellow believers.

Imagine how life would have been different if Eve had not been alone as a woman — if a few discerning girlfriends had been around to keep her accountable. If she'd had some mature friends in whom to confide, the history of the human race might have been altered. The scenario might have looked something like this:

Eve: "Slick Serpent Satan says all I have to do to be as smart as God is to take one little bite from that luscious fruit fenced off in the middle of the Garden."

Girlfriend 1: "Evie, Evie, Evie. Don't even think about it! If it sounds too good to be true, it undoubtedly is."

Girlfriend 2: "Listen, sister, go back and tell that wily slitherer to hit the road before you stretch him into a nice handbag and matching shoes."

Unfortunately for Eve, she didn't have those girlfriends. Even though she had clear, precise instructions from God, Eve and her husband dirtied their perfect relationship with Him and each other, forcing God to let them go their "own way."

Centuries later, we are still wondering why relationships are difficult, complicated, and often contentious. In so many different contexts—dating, marriage, friendships, work, church—we continually struggle to live at peace with one another.

Still, God has not given up on us. He has graciously offered another way for us to learn how to cultivate healthy, strong, mutually satisfying relationships. He inspired the apostle Paul to explain to Titus the importance of older women teaching younger women through their own life experiences: "Then [the older women] can train the younger women to love their husbands and children, to be self-controlled and pure, to be busy at home, to be kind, and to be subject to their husbands, so that no one will malign the word of God" (Titus 2:4-5). By allowing older, more seasoned women to walk alongside us, we gain wisdom, insight, and encouragement in critical areas of life.

If you have already found a more experienced, loving friend to meet with regularly, that's great! Thank the Lord for the opportunity to learn from a woman who has "been there." We suggest that you and your mentor use this book to explore important faith issues and stimulate discussions.

Still, we know that most women in our society, which fosters isolation and transitory relationships, don't have a mentor, teacher, guide, confidante, or older friend. If you are one of those still searching and praying for help and guidance, we invite you to join our circle of friends and find it in this book.

Permit us to serve as your guides, encouragers, and cheerleaders for spiritual growth and maturity. Our intent is to fulfill God's plan—as outlined in Titus 2—for older, more seasoned women to come alongside those younger or less experienced and help them grow in their faith and relationships.

As you read and study individually or in a group, we will walk with you, encourage you, laugh with you, and cry with you. Your load will feel lighter, and we hope you will have the new awareness that you are not alone. Someone does care. Come join us as we endeavor to empower you throughout this book by using the words of Titus 2:4-5 and our own personal experiences.

WOMEN, WE'RE IN THIS TOGETHER!

Our Failures, Heartaches, and Struggles

BY ANGIE CONRAD, PAM MILLER, TAMMY
EAGAN, SANDY KERSHAW,
AND JANET COX

S ometimes life is hard. We all know how to look good on the outside, even when things are crumbling. For a time, we can appear to have everything under control. The majority of the people we encounter see only a tiny slice of our lives, and we can make that slice look great. Our marriage, our children, our career, and even our wardrobe can appear polished and well managed from a distance. But we dare not let anyone look too closely. Perhaps you can relate to Jenny's story. . . .

⌣ ◇ ⌢

Jenny fought back tears as she sat alone in the church pew and scanned the familiar faces around her. She knew that comparing herself with others was dangerous, but she couldn't help wondering if others ever experienced the same hollow, restless feeling that gnawed at her.

As Jenny looked around, her attention was primarily drawn to the women. She couldn't imagine that Sarah, sitting a few rows in front of her, had ever had a bad day. With her bright smile, Sarah brought warmth to any setting and always greeted everyone cheerfully. Looking at Sarah, it would be hard to believe her third child was only six weeks old. She seemed to have the energy of a teenager and the figure to match.

How can life be so effortless for people like Sarah? Jenny asked herself.

Across the aisle, Jenny observed Karen sitting close to her husband in their usual spot. He had his arm around Karen as if to say, "I'm so proud of my beautiful wife." Jenny wondered what it would be like to have a husband who shared her newfound faith. She pictured families like Karen's huddled in the living room as they prayed and read Bible stories together. Jenny found it hard to imagine Karen ever feeling the deep loneliness that she felt on a daily basis.

Earlier that morning, Claire, her daughter's Sunday school teacher, had greeted Jenny. Jenny sensed Claire's disapproval as she attempted to break her four-year-old's grip on her right thigh. She felt as if everyone were watching this weekly ritual. It was hard to imagine one of Claire's teenage boys causing a scene. Claire had been the model stay-at-home mom while Jenny's job required her to leave her children in day care three days a week. Even though Claire was always kind, Jenny sensed that behind her warm greeting was a litany of unspoken advice on how Jenny might improve her parenting skills.

These were Jenny's perceptions on that Sunday morning. She saw only a sliver of the lives of these people all dressed up in their Sunday best. Jenny's observations were full of assumptions. Her ideas about the lives of others were filtered through her own desires and insecurities. As she was hopelessly drawn into the pit of comparison, she felt even more lonely and isolated from the women who could have been such a help to her.

If only she could spend more time with them and know that they struggle, too—some in ways that would shock her. But busyness, pride, and fear keep Jenny from really getting to know the other women.

What would happen if all the masks were laid aside? What if Jenny and her fellow parishioners could see each other when they weren't at their best? What if Jenny knew that the effervescent Sarah was trying desperately to hold her marriage together and that her enviable figure was not the result of self-discipline but stress-related health problems? And what if Jenny understood that Sarah, fearing she would soon be raising her three children alone, had spent the morning scanning the classified ads in search of a better-paying job?

What a difference it would make if Jenny knew that Claire actually admired her commitment and resolve to bring her children to church each week while managing her home and career. In fact, now that Claire has teenagers, she longs for the uncomplicated days when her children were young.

If only Jenny could follow Karen and her Prince Charming home that afternoon, she'd see the pile of bills on their kitchen counter and hear the anger in his voice as he took out his frustration on Karen and their kids. Jenny would have learned that even seemingly "put-together" Christian couples fall on hard times and struggle in their relationships.

Life is really much the same for each of these women. The circumstances and details of their problems may be different, but they share similar challenges, disappointments, heartaches, and failures. And if they only knew how alike they really were, they could support one another and learn from one another.

In this book, we offer you that kind of opportunity. No matter how "together" we look (or sound), we want you to realize that we've struggled, too, and we want to share with you what we've learned as a result. As you read the following stories, you'll see we are not perfect—in fact, we're more ordinary than extraordinary. Underneath our "Sunday best" are struggles just like yours.

Angie's Story

As I gaze down at my forty-five-year-old knees, I am reminded that the scars and calluses from falling during my life's journey may not be pretty, but they are well deserved. As I was growing up from birth to double digits (age ten), my family continually moved from city to city and state to state. My father joined the Army when I was a baby, and it seemed that my entire early childhood was spent settling into new neighborhoods and schools. I know what it feels like not to have neighborhood roots and to struggle constantly to make new friends. My anxiety level reached a fevered pitch around the age of eight. My desire for a close friend made my heart ache.

Eventually, all the relocating did stop, but not for a positive reason: we stopped moving because my father was killed in action in Vietnam.

A sense of abandonment became my constant—and loathsome—companion. In addition to all of the turmoil and grief that accompanies the loss of a parent, if religion had brought me any comfort up to that point, it had abandoned me. I had been taught that God was out to punish me for any and all of my indiscretions, and I came to believe that my father's death was just one more way God was punishing me.

My insecurities mounted, but I hid them well. Indeed, I was a master of disguises during my adolescence and young adulthood. The pain in my life was temporarily assuaged by experimentation with marijuana, alcohol, and relationships.

Fortunately for me, in my late twenties I allowed the gaping hole in my life to be filled with a relationship with Jesus. My spiritual and emotional growth did not occur swiftly and smoothly, of course. I endured many "growing pains"—and still do, as I learn to follow God's path.

I know I would not be able to help you on your spiritual journey if I hadn't first failed and then grabbed onto the outstretched hands of loving, more experienced women throughout my lifetime. These godly mentors and role models affectionately administered first aid to my emotional and spiritual scrapes and bruises.

Fifteen years ago, I found myself desperately in need of such women. Have you ever heard of Epidermolysis Bullosa? My husband and I hadn't either until we were blessed with a beautiful baby boy we named Andy. When blisters started forming on his feet and hands, we became concerned. We noticed that they healed within several days but left scars. How strange! It took six weeks of going from doctor to doctor before we finally discovered that Andy had an incurable skin disorder and was missing the anchoring fibrils that hold his layers of skin together. Not only had we never heard of this disease, but due to its rarity, the doctors didn't know much about it either. My husband and I dove into researching it and found that, in many cases, there are so many complications from scarring and pain that the disease is fatal.

At the time, I was a "baby" Christian who had a yearning to know Jesus personally but knew zilch about the

Bible. I begged God to give me help in taking care of my baby and understanding why this had happened to our new little family. I mustered my courage and joined my first small-group Bible study at the church I had been attending. I asked the church child-care workers to muster *their* courage to take care of Andy while I participated in the study. I knew they were scared to death of touching my baby for fear of hurting him, but they agreed to give me a break and allow me to build relationships with other Christian women.

I appeared bold to others, but I felt terribly insecure. I had hardly cracked a Bible in my lifetime, and I had never discussed Scripture with a group of women I didn't know (and whom I assumed were much more godly than I was). But God knew what He was doing when He led me there, and I found my first mentors in that group.

Even though doctors assured my husband and me that the chances of having another child with the disease were practically nonexistent, our second son, Sam, was born with no skin on his left leg and a severe deformity of his left foot because of Epidermolysis Bullosa. Paula, a friend from the group, was there for me. Though her husband was very ill with leukemia, she came from his hospital bedside to help me bandage Sam's leg for the first time at my home. As Sam lay screaming at the top of his lungs in pain, Paula held my hand and said, "Angie, we're going to get through this together. I'm here for you." Her husband died of leukemia a few months later.

I still cry, twelve years later, when I think about God's great design of women helping women and the blessing of brave and encouraging friends like Paula, who have helped me to learn to deal with the unfairness and absurdities of life with faith, courage, and determination. Even though they appeared to be more spiritual than I was (my assessment, not theirs), they were actually just like you and me.

They were willing to let God use their experience to guide and mentor me, a woman in need. Now God is allowing me to use my experience, pain, and growth to help you. Could we possibly have a more loving, ingenious God?

Pam's Story

New Year's Eve 1975 will forever be etched in my memory. Everyone around me was celebrating the New Year while I sat alone in front of the television watching that huge ball drop in Times Square as Guy Lombardo's band played. No one knew how desperate I felt—desperate to the point of contemplating suicide.

Raising my eyes to heaven in despair, I sobbed, "Is this all there is to life? Is it worth it to go on?"

As a troubled teenager, I had been insecure and plagued by low self-esteem. I tried filling the void I felt with alcohol, drugs, and boys. These would only give me temporary happiness; I'd then come crashing down again to reality—and emptiness.

During my senior year in high school, the inner turmoil grew. I lacked purpose and direction in my life, and the nagging feeling of desperation and loneliness was so strong that I thought I would implode. How I wished someone would come alongside me to care for me, go below the surface, and reach the person I really was. No one knew the pain I was feeling because I successfully disguised it. I was at the end of my rope and cried, "Is there anyone out there who cares?"

Little did I know that God heard my cries for help and sent a friend, Jeanine. The next day, she invited me to visit her church youth group. In the past when she had invited me, I'd scoffed. This time I was desperate, so I said yes.

Walking into the meeting, I instantly saw a difference in those kids' lives. I was drawn to them because I sensed they had "something" I didn't. That evening I asked Jeanine lots of questions, wanting to understand "the meaning of life" they all seemed to have. Jeanine explained how God loved me so much that He sent His Son to die on the cross for my sins. I definitely knew I was a sinner and needed a savior.

Maybe this is what I've been searching for, I thought. *No wonder I couldn't find "the missing piece" in my life. It's Jesus I need to make me whole.*

The search was over! I eagerly prayed and asked Jesus to be my personal Savior. That day I felt deep joy and peace like I had never experienced before. The meaning of life started to become clear to me. I wanted to grow in my personal relationship with Christ and to tell others about Him.

I was hungry to learn all I could about the Bible and my new relationship with Christ. At Bowling Green State University in Ohio, I was involved with The Navigators, an interdenominational Christian organization. Through The Navigators, I met Diane and Carol, who were older college students. They were godly women whom I respected. They came alongside to help me learn how to study the Bible, pray, and share my faith. Best of all, they were friends I knew cared about me.

Later I met Karen, Kathy, and Teri through The Navigators' community ministry in the Chicago area. These mature Christian women encouraged me and pointed out qualities and spiritual gifts God was developing in my life. It was during that time that I started growing in confidence, because I knew they believed in me. I thought, *Maybe I do have something to offer others.*

Because of these women's example and support, I began working with teens in my church's youth group. Vividly remembering my own difficult teen years, I prayed, "God use me to encourage these teens, guide them, care about them, and help them grow in their faith."

God answered my simple prayer. For the next nine years I spent much time with teenage girls. I became their "spiritual mom," challenging them to grow in their relationships with Christ, helping them sort out decisions, and gently guiding them down the right path. What a joy to see each of these girls mentor a younger girl in the youth group—spiritual multiplication in action!

After I moved to East Peoria, Illinois, in 1986, I married Kevin and we started a family. My passion to reach out and help others grow was still strong, but now God had redirected that passion from teens to young moms. In my church, I began leading a moms' group and informally mentoring them. Many of us had young children, so we easily connected. Not only did our children benefit by developing their social skills, but we moms did, too. Our conversations would encompass a wide range of topics, from spiritual growth to child discipline, from time management to strengthening our marriages. Coming away from our times together, we would each feel rejuvenated and motivated in our roles as wives, mothers, and Christians.

Now, twelve years later, this group still meets occasionally. We continue to see the group as a safe haven for sharing our struggles and joys with each other. Our discussion topics have changed a bit from our first meeting days, but our desire remains the same: to balance work, home, and ministry; to keep "the flame" alive with our husbands; and to grow in our relationships with Christ. Our conversations are always encouraging, stimulating, challenging, and educational. It's amazing how much we learn from each other's experiences and insights.

While it's a challenge to get together in the midst of busy schedules, the rewards are great. And what are the rewards? Encouragement and motivation to press on; renewed desire to be the best wives, moms, and Christians we can be; practical help in a struggle we may be having; guidance in our relationships; and simply the joy of getting together and laughing until our sides hurt.

God definitely did not desire for us to be alone. Relationships are *key* to our growth as individuals and as Christians. It is undoubtedly worth the time and sacrifice to keep our relationships growing and strong.

Tammy's Story

As I opened the bathroom medicine cabinet, the pills my doctor had just prescribed mockingly glared at me.

"Depression has a physiological as well as psychological component," my physician had calmly stated earlier that day. "Antidepressants aren't a quick fix, but they will regulate the chemical deficiencies you are experiencing. This will make your counseling sessions more effective."

I had a week to consider whether I would take them while I waited for the results of some preliminary blood tests. Whatever my decision about the medicine, I knew something had to be done. I was desperate. I was willing to try anything to feel normal again. How had life so completely unraveled for a twenty-eight-year-old wife and mother of two adorable children?

I learned early on that it feels good when people like you, and it hurts when they don't. For all of us, life is sprinkled with both criticism and applause. For me, it seemed that no matter how much affection I received, it didn't stick. Like rain on waterproof clothing, any affirmation from family and friends rolled off me. Yet anything that was hurtful or humiliating seemed to saturate my soul and fill me with a deep sense of shame. From my earliest years, I felt unlovable and unlovely. And yet something within my spirit set out to do battle with those feelings. Perhaps by convincing others that I was lovable, I could also convince myself.

I was fortunate to discover Jesus' love for me at age thirteen. But by the time I entered my suburban Chicago high school, the newness of my faith had worn thin. I found it difficult to find my footing as a young Christian. There were many things much more appealing that would give me the approval I craved, so I aggressively pursued them.

If there was a vocal or musical group, I tried out; a class office, I ran for it; a club or society, I joined it. When I made the cheerleading squad, I felt I had reached the pinnacle of American high school success. Life was full of dances, football games, and homecoming parades, where instead of watching from the sidelines, I enjoyed the ride at center stage. However, popularity had its dark side that was often hidden from parents and teachers.

After high school, a move to a new city provided an opportunity to leave behind my "socialite" lifestyle and get back to my faith. The early 1980s was the era of the "superChristian." Contemporary Christian music was flourishing, and the album covers portrayed the smiling, clean-cut faces of those who crooned about the perfect Christian life. Bookstores were full of testimonies from superstar athletes who were out to win the world for Christ. Though these Christians were quite sincere, most only put their best face forward and rarely discussed their struggles and failures. These Christian celebrities became a replacement for the cheerleaders and popular kids I'd always admired—and tried to be.

Thus the curtain was drawn, and I entered a new stage of playing the part of the perfect Christian single . . . then wife . . . then mother.

All of this contributed to the day I stared into the medicine cabinet and wondered how life had become so unmanageable. Though I had decided I would take the antidepressants, a blood test revealed some surprising results that prevented this. My husband and I received the happy news that baby number three was well on his way, and thankfully I had not taken a single dose of a medication that could have harmed him. The pregnancy provided the perfect opportunity to bring my life to a screeching halt and spend an entire two years primarily taking care of myself and my family.

During this time, God rescued me through long, quiet days of relative solitude (as much solitude as one can have with three young children). He also sent some imperfect yet amazing women into my life to minister to me. Many were there all along, but I was too busy to listen to them, learn from them, and see them as they really were. Some may have no idea what a gift they were as they affirmed and challenged me.

A year ago I celebrated the milestone of turning forty. What a joyful day! I like the woman I see in the mirror (even though she is definitely older and quite a bit rounder). I'm happy with who I am. I couldn't have come to this point by myself. God used my relationships with the women around me to transform my life through their love and example.

Although I don't often dwell on the past, as a forty-year-old woman I would love to revisit my twenty-eight-year-old self. There are so many things I would like to teach her, so much pain I would like to spare her. Because of what I have received, I want to share what I learned with you.

Sandy's Story

How do you roast a twenty-pound turkey? What ingredients go into the stuffing? Twenty-four years ago, I didn't know about the Butterball turkey hotline. And I wanted my Christmas turkey and stuffing to taste like my mother's. She had died unexpectedly that October of a brain aneurysm, so that first Christmas without her was going to be difficult. As the oldest child in my family, I was going to attempt to "fill in" for my mother by preparing Christmas dinner for my father, sister, brother, their spouses, and my husband and children.

I had helped my mother with previous holiday dinners, but she had been in charge of the turkey and stuffing. As a youngster, my job had been to tear the bread (my mother's method for stuffing mix), but I had never actually blended together the other ingredients. I drew on my memory and checked the ingredients in a cookbook to see if I was close, in hopes of duplicating the taste of my mother's recipe. For help with the turkey, I called a close friend.

"Don't ask me," she replied. "I've never cooked a turkey. My mother always does that part."

So I did it alone.

Want to know how that all-important family Christmas dinner turned out? My brother and his wife ended up going somewhere else. My sister's husband came down with a bad case of respiratory flu, so they didn't come either. Only my father came. Then, to make matters worse, I inadvertently set the oven on "broil," so the turkey browned beautifully but was not done inside when we sat down to eat. I realized my mistake and changed the oven to "bake." We ate the turkey and stuffing as our dessert.

Over the years as I've faced the challenges of being a wife and mother, I've had other questions I wished my mom could answer: How could you be so brave as to let me walk eight blocks to school as a first-grader without even watching me? (I needed to let my daughter, Kristin, go only two blocks, and I still worried.) How were you able to calmly send me to the store on icy streets only two days after I received my driver's license? (Kristin drove alone for the first time in fine summer weather.) How did you cope with loneliness and the neediness of small children when

Dad was away so much? (Occasionally, my husband, Steve, was gone four to six days a month.) Many times I have reached for the phone to share my thoughts and feelings with my mom, only to remember she wouldn't be at the end of the line.

So who could I turn to? I had no close aunts. My mother-in-law lived on the East Coast, as did my sisters-in-law. Unfortunately, we didn't have close relationships with each other. I did not know my neighbors well; in fact, I rarely saw them. It seemed natural to turn to older women I knew in my church. They answered my occasional questions, but I never knew any of them well enough to say, "I miss my mother—her advice, wisdom, companionship, and encouragement. Would you consider letting me come to *you* for help when I need it?"

I recognized that I didn't necessarily need an *older* woman, just one with more experience. So I turned to friends who fit this description. Over and over, Debbie, Jan, and I muddled through our problems together, helping and encouraging one another in spiritual matters and daily challenges. These friends walked alongside me, and we grew together as we shared our lives.

As I've gotten older, I have often felt compassion for young women who no longer have their mothers or who live too far from them and need a more experienced friend.

We need other women in our lives! They can't take the place of God or our mothers or our husbands, but they can fill relational needs that we have. Spending time with other women is, as the Titus 2 passage reminds us, part of God's design. It is a responsibility, but also a privilege.

Janet's Story

Betty was one of those people everyone could relate to in some way. Reaching out to others in need came naturally to her. She was a single forty-two-year-old who enjoyed her career in accounting. I met her about forty years ago, when I started my first "real" job at The Pillsbury Company in the big city of Minneapolis. At that point, I was investigating Christianity but not yet convinced that it was the best thing for me.

During one of my occasional visits to church, a person had given me a little booklet of Bible verses, which I kept on my desk at work. Betty saw it when she retrieved some papers from my desk and assumed I would be open to talking about Christianity. Almost every Monday morning, she would stop by my desk early to chat. At first she would inquire in subtle ways about my relationship with Christ. Later she asked how I had spent my weekend and if I had attended church. She was not prying but was just interested in helping me learn and grow in faith. Sometimes she would share a Scripture verse or an interesting story about her walk with Jesus.

Very gently she would point out how our coworker Marci was dressing in a way that attracted the wrong kind of people into her life. Not coincidentally, I quit wearing some of my really short skirts to work. Betty mentioned that late-night carousing kept Marci from doing her job well and as a result prevented her from getting a promotion. I cut out the late-night parties and got to bed earlier. Betty was clearly pointing out a better way of life.

Over nine months, Betty's gentle spirit continually demonstrated to me that she cared. It was in the fall of 1963 that I opened my heart to Christ. A few months later, Marci, who was my age, came up missing. Her loose and impure lifestyle was her undoing. I often tell my family when we see a person suffering from a lifetime of wrong choices, "There but for the grace of God go I."

Betty was faithful in being there for me, answering my questions, and praying for me. She was the mentor I needed at that time.

Arlene was a Christian neighbor I met years later when my children were going through the challenging teen and preteen years. They were eleven, twelve, fourteen, and fifteen at the time. It was all I could do to keep up with them and their activities. Arlene's children were grown and doing well, so I knew she had learned a lot along the way. The advice I most often heard from older women was, "This too shall pass!" Arlene was different in that she would listen to my "struggle of the day" and give concrete answers. She, like Betty, had the heart of a mentor and took the time to walk with me through my struggles.

The apostle Paul gave Titus instructions for the older women to teach the younger ones in matters like these: self-control, purity, kindness, and relational issues involving their husbands and children. These topics can be overwhelming if we first read them and then endeavor to cover all of these areas at once. They need explanation. They need to be fleshed out in the life of someone we know and respect—and that's the beauty of the Titus 2 passage. We weren't meant to walk alone through life's journey. I benefited greatly from the influence of Betty, Arlene, and other women who passed along their wisdom and experience. I'm delighted to share with you a few things I've learned.

The list of topics found in Titus 2:4-5 form the outline for this book. Even though the lessons we have learned don't always fit into one neat little package, this book should be like leaven—a starter to direct you down a path of cultivating healthy relationships and godly character.

Draw on our life experiences. Take advantage of where we have been! Let us encourage you, motivate you, guide you, and challenge you in your relationship with Christ and others. Grow with us as we share with you.

DIGGING DEEPER

1. Make a list of qualities you look for in a woman you want to learn from. Take time to pray right now that God would bring such a woman into your life. (For more information, see appendix A, "How to Find a Mentor.")

2. Think back over your lifetime. List the women who have come alongside you and had a positive impact on your life.

3. What is your biggest fear about opening yourself to friendships in mentoring relationships with other women?

4. What do the following Scripture passages communicate to you about Jesus being your friend and mentor?
Luke 9:18-21

Luke 9:41

Luke 9:57-62

Luke 10:1-18

Luke 19:41

John 11:17-35

What do you learn from the above Scriptures concerning the ways you can help others?

5. What instructions are we given in 2 Timothy 2:2 for making mentoring an ongoing activity?

How can you utilize these instructions in your own neighborhood or community?

6. Read and meditate on 1 Thessalonians 2:7-12.
   a. What is the relationship Paul has with the Thessalonians?

   b. Read verses 7 and 11 and contrast the role of a nursing mother to that of the role of a father.

   c. Using a dictionary or Bible reference book, look up and explain in your own words what it means to:
   exhort

   encourage

   implore

    d. How are these words the same? How are they different?

7. What was the reason or goal Paul had in mind for this kind of teaching/learning relationship with the Thessalonians?

Chapter One

STEPPING BACK IN TIME

What Did Paul Really Say About Women?

BY TAMMY EAGAN

Then [the older women] can train the younger
women to love their husbands and children, to be
self-controlled and pure, to be busy at home, to be
kind, and to be subject to their husbands, so that no
one will malign the word of God.

Titus 2:4-5

A Christian magazine once published a cartoon that
reflects the way our culture views some of the
teachings of the Bible, including the writings of
the apostle Paul. The sketch featured Paul arriving by boat
and being met by an angry mob of women. They held
signs saying, "Unfair to women!" and "Paul is a male
chauvinist pig!" The caption below the sketch quotes
"Paul": "Heh, heh. I see you got my letter!"[1]

In our times, some churches have been criticized when
it comes to their views on issues affecting women. Biblical

teachings about submission in marriage and the value of the home and motherhood have been taken out of context and perceived to limit or devalue women. However, a comprehensive look at the scriptural message reveals a different perspective.

In contrast to what the church's critics say, others have said that nothing in the history of the world has done more to elevate the status of women than Christianity. In order to appreciate this point of view, we need to have our vision adjusted. Our eyes have adapted to seeing the world according to the standards of the only culture most of us have experienced—modern Western society. To get a good perspective on what the Bible says, it is helpful to examine it in a new way.

The teachings of Scripture are most clear when we are looking through the right "glasses" or context—the culture and values of the first century. This was the world in which Jesus and Paul lived and taught. Their teachings transcend all cultures and all times, but twenty-first-century readers gain greater appreciation for their lives and ministries as we understand the customs, mores, and traditions of their day. With our vision enhanced, we will see what amazing and radical love God has for His people, including women.

This is particularly important as we set out to discuss the issues listed in Titus 2:4-5. Without any background about the circumstances surrounding these verses and without understanding a little about the culture in New Testament times, we might find these verses hard to digest. To our minds, these admonitions look more like a life sentence than a life-giving opportunity. To appreciate the value of Titus 2 to our world today, let's look at a slice of life during the time it was written.

The Role of Women in Jesus' Time

Let's begin by looking back at the religious and social structure of Jesus' day. New Testament scholars provide us with a sketch of how women were often viewed and treated. Women were secluded from public life as much as possible. With the exception of their wedding day, it was shameful for them to be seen publicly with their faces uncovered. Touching or speaking to a woman in public was taboo for the devout Jewish man, especially if he was a religious leader. Sometimes, even in the home, men and women were strictly segregated. It was reported that in very stringent homes, it was possible for a boy to grow up without seeing his mother's face.

A first-century Jewish woman was considered to have the same status as a slave or a piece of property owned first by her father, then by her husband. A father could sell his daughter into slavery until she was twelve years old. After that, he could give her in marriage to the man of his choosing, as long as the man could meet the dowry price the father demanded. The woman typically had no voice in these decisions.

What's more, a man could divorce his wife for even a minor offense. He could also invite another wife or concubine into the home, and the first wife was expected to welcome her without question. In the event of an emergency, the fathers and sons were saved first, then the daughters, and the women last.

Women were greatly restricted in public religious practices. They could attend a portion of the worship at the synagogue as long as they remained unseen behind a lattice screen, out of the view of the worshiping men. Women were to maintain absolute silence during worship. They were kept uneducated lest they learn to read and gain access to the Law. They were forbidden from hearing, let alone discussing or teaching, the Word of God. One rabbi said, "It would be better that the Torah be burnt than to be spoken from the lips of a woman."[2]

A popular prayer at the time stated, "Blessed be He [God] who did not make me a Gentile, a dog, a woman."[3] The order in which women are placed in that series tells us a lot! There were, of course, exceptions to the cultural norms, and some women were given greater status in the family. However, the conditions described above were not unusual.

Jesus Honors Women

Into this picture enters Jesus. Over and over again we read of His face-to-face interactions with women. He prayed for them and healed them. He commended them for their faith. He touched them, and they touched Him. Such episodes recorded in the Bible don't seem quite so unusual through our twenty-first-century eyes, but in Jesus' time they were astounding.

One such incident, found in Luke 10:38-42, is an encounter at the home of Mary and Martha. Jesus and His disciples were the guests, and the women, sisters Martha and Mary, were serving them. Mary did an unusual thing—she sat at Jesus' feet, listening to His teaching. Even more amazing, Jesus welcomed her. When Martha complained that all the serving had fallen on her, Jesus commended Mary for making the best choice.

In the Gospels we read of how this same compelling love gave a woman with unresolved bleeding (an "unclean" condition, according to the Law) the courage to quietly touch Jesus' garment, believing that she would be healed after twelve years of bleeding. At that time, it was not permitted for a woman who was bleeding to have any social interaction—let alone to *touch* a religious leader. She might have approached Him with timidity and fear, yet Jesus commended her great faith.

Remember also that it was women who were among the last to watch Him die and the first at His tomb. They came to care for His body. Instead, they were privileged to be the first to witness the Resurrection. What honor Jesus placed on the women that day. They were even appointed to tell the men!

Paul Values Women

Now let's fast-forward a few years and look at the ministry of the apostle Paul, who wrote the majority of the New Testament epistles. Paul described his life before his encounter with Jesus: "According to the strictest sect of our religion, I lived as a Pharisee" (Acts 26:5). This was the same religion of Jesus' day. However, we see evidence that after his conversion, Paul gave women the same kind of respect that Jesus did. He valued them as fellow workers in ministry. He relied upon them. He taught men how to treat them and encouraged husbands to greatly value their wives to the point of sacrifice, just as Christ had given Himself for His bride, the church.

Although it is merely speculation, I would guess that the women of Paul's day did not see him as the great oppressor of women illustrated in the cartoon described earlier. They probably warmly embraced him and rejoiced in the way he honored them by making provision for them to be taught and to take part in the work of the kingdom. Indeed, Paul must have ruffled some religious feathers when he proclaimed that in Christ "there is neither Jew nor Greek, there is neither slave nor free man, there is neither male nor female; for you are all one in Christ Jesus" (Galatians 3:28, NASB).

As I look at Paul's words in the last chapter of the

book of Romans, I wonder what it would have been like to be Phoebe—to be commended by Paul for being such a great help to many people, including Paul himself. If I were Priscilla, would I have been surprised to see Paul list my name even before my husband's and call us *both* fellow workers in Christ Jesus?

Without a clear view of the culture of the New Testament, we might be oblivious to the fact that Paul's actions and ideas were radically freeing for the people to whom he spoke. Paul and others were ultimately killed for speaking God's truth. Some of the anger wrought against them was enflamed by their courage to proclaim that God's grace was available to all who believed, including women and others who previously had been excluded from active participation in religious activities.

A Closer Look at Titus 2:4-5

Paul's letter to Titus is part of a section of the New Testament referred to as the Pastoral Epistles. The Pastoral Epistles include 1 Timothy, 2 Timothy, and Titus, which Paul wrote toward the end of his life and ministry. They provide the best glimpse into Paul's practice in organizing the leadership of the church as he teaches two young pastors, Timothy and Titus, how to deal with troubled churches.

Titus was assigned to a struggling church in Crete, which lies directly south of the Aegean Sea and is the fourth largest island in the Mediterranean. The people of Crete were prosperous due to their agriculture and trade. Unfortunately, the conduct of the people in the churches of Crete was less than honorable. In Titus 1:12, we read of their reputation for dishonesty, laziness, and gluttony. Titus was asked to raise the standard for Christian conduct among these people.

In the second chapter, Paul instructs Titus to promote good character and teaching by developing strong, godly leaders in the church. Paul gives encouragement and specific admonition to older men, older women, young women, young men, and slaves.

One of Paul's proposals, found in Titus 2:4-5, is that younger women learn from older, more spiritually mature women about important life issues—family relationships and character development. Both should reflect the Word of God in a positive way.

Dr. Gary W. Demarest points out that some may "pounce" on these verses because they seem to assert that "a woman's place is in the home and that God created women to be subservient to men."[4] At first glance, it may appear that one would have a case for such an argument as these verses make no mention of women in the workplace or pursuing interests outside the home. This is a time for putting on our first-century glasses and looking at the culture in which Paul was writing. Demarest says, "In Crete, at the time of this writing, young women had no option to marriage and motherhood. As far as we can tell, the only employment for a young woman outside of the home was as a prostitute on the streets or in a pagan temple."[5] The commentator does mention Lydia from Thyatira, who was a businesswoman, but points out that she was probably an older woman with grown children.

Theologian John R. W. Stott clearly lays any controversy to rest as he states, "What he [Paul] is opposing is not a wife's pursuit of a profession but the habit of being idle and going about from house to house."[6] It is no more logical to understand Titus 2:4-5 as stifling the modern career woman than it would be to see verses 9 and 10 as promoting slavery in today's culture. Both scenarios describe the common cultural conditions of the time. Yet the heart of the teaching within the passage is relevant to all times.

The Tradition Continues

The New Testament model of young women learning from older women still applies today, even though some of the methods have changed. Loving your husband today might include sending him an encouraging e-mail or driving a minivan full of kids across town to buy him a special gift. Loving your children might include sacrificing your own career to care for them full time at home. That sacrificial love could also mean working outside the home to help provide for your family while ensuring that household duties are not neglected.

It is not necessary to view the list of virtues found in Titus 2:4-5 as an exhaustive one. It also need not be an *exhausting* list! We cannot master all these character traits at once; they take a lifetime. We may learn about these issues at different times in our lives from many different women. Some lessons may come easily and some may need to be practiced over and over.

Hopefully, this book will be a launching pad for experiencing the encouragement that comes from spending time with other women. In our culture, women no longer work side by side in the tasks of caring for their families and growing in their walks with God. We have to be more *intentional* about making time to encourage one another, no matter what our stage of life.

You may have a rich, growing faith in Christ and may be familiar with the Bible. Or you may be just beginning to explore Christianity. You might not be sure if you believe the Bible *is* God's Word, but are eager to find out. You may be working through these lessons with a group or tackling them on your own. You are to be commended for making time for this in your busy life. And you have something in common with other readers of this book: God is at work in your life, drawing you to a deeper relationship with Him—or you wouldn't be reading it.

Don't Forget the Grace

One final word of instruction: Don't forget about God's love, which I spoke of in the beginning of this chapter. Remember how Jesus welcomed Mary when she broke away from her busyness and sat at His feet? That same compelling love beckons and receives you just as you are. This great love also empowers you to live a Titus 2:4-5 life. Paul himself draws attention to this issue as he reminds Titus:

> It wasn't so long ago that we ourselves were stupid and stubborn, dupes of sin, ordered every which way by our glands, going around with a chip on our shoulder, hated and hating back. But when God, our kind and loving Savior God, stepped in, he saved us from all that. It was all his doing; we had nothing to do with it. He gave us a good bath, and we came out of it new people, washed inside and out by the Holy Spirit. Our Savior Jesus poured out new life so generously. God's gift has restored our relationship with him and given us back our lives. And there's more life to come—an eternity of life! (Titus 3:3-7, MSG)

The topics of these chapters are areas women find most dear to their hearts. They are also arenas where we are likely to feel we don't measure up. Keep in mind that you are in a *process* of growth. Growth only happens as you draw close to God and allow Him to transform you into the woman He wants you to be. We all fall and might have to get up again many times. Falling is not failure. We only fail when we lose hope, lack trust, or refuse to take action on what God shows us. We must always submerge ourselves in God's love and forgiveness.

DIGGING DEEPER

1. Have you ever wondered if some of the teachings of the Bible or the church reflect a sexist view toward women? If so, what specific teachings?

2. Read Luke 10:38-42. For what is Mary commended by Jesus? What are some possible explanations for Mary's behavior?

3. Read Luke 8:26-56.
   a. Compare the way the woman who was bleeding approached Jesus to the way others approached Him in this same chapter.

b. What kinds of feelings do you think this woman might have experienced before Jesus healed her?

c. How do you think she felt after Jesus healed her?

4. Read Luke 8:1-3. In addition to the twelve apostles, who else traveled with Jesus?

5. Read Galatians 3:26-28 and Genesis 1:27. What do men and women have in common in these verses?

6. Do you tend to feel inferior to men in general? What about men in the church? Has this negatively affected your spiritual life? If so, how?

7. Have you assumed that God values men more than women? If so, how has that affected your faith and walk with God?

8. Read Romans 16:1-15. List the women Paul mentions. For what qualities does Paul commend these women?

9. If you had lived in New Testament times, how might Paul's ministry have impacted your life?

10. Read Paul's entire letter to Titus. Answer the following:
    a. To whom is Paul writing?

    b. What is Paul's relationship to the recipient?

c. Consider Paul as a mentor to Titus. On what topics does Paul instruct Titus?

d. Who are the groups of people Titus will instruct?

e. What changes does Paul hope to see in the people of Crete?

11. Multiple choice: Paul expects lives to change because of
   a. Good preaching at Sunday services.
   b. Titus's personal example.
   c. Paul's personal example.
   d. Teaching or mentoring that happens on a day-to-day basis within the various groups of people.

Chapter Two

A LEARNED SKILL

Loving Your Husband

BY SANDY KERSHAW

Then [the older women] can train the younger
women to love their husbands.

Titus 2:4

"Why don't you just pack up your little red
Volkswagen and leave!"

They were words—my words—spoken
in anger and frustration. My husband, Steve, and I were
having another argument about something so insignificant that neither of us can recall the issue at this point.
My "suggestion" for him to leave hung in the air
between us. We glared at each other . . . and then burst
out laughing!

Steve and I became good friends at Monmouth
College in Monmouth, Illinois, never thinking we would
fall in love and marry. We were wrong—after a couple
years of being *just friends,* we did fall in love and eventually married. And because we were friends first, we

thought we would avoid the typical marriage problems. Wrong again!

In the early years of our marriage, we argued about all kinds of small matters. For example, Steve liked to sleep late most Saturdays, getting up at eleven o'clock or noon. I thought that was a waste of the morning. Many times I would "sleep in" until eight or nine, then head to the Laundromat, adopting my best Joan of Arc attitude. If Steve was still sleeping when I returned to our apartment, my anger would rise another degree or two. Once he was up, I would greet my cheery husband with an icy demeanor and a frosty hello. I wanted him to know how I felt about his sleeping in.

I thought Steve would know why I was upset, but he didn't have a clue! It took many such episodes before I realized I needed to *tell* him how I felt. I learned that husbands can't read their wives' minds. Once I learned to share my thoughts, many unpleasant situations were avoided.

Other misunderstandings stemmed not from *what* Steve said, but *how* he said it: "How in the world could you . . . ?" Or, "Whatever possessed you to . . . ?" Or, "I can't believe you . . . !" These were not actual inquiries but accusations, and I thought they were insensitive and unkind. Frustrated and hurt, I would cry and try to explain myself . . . and Steve would ignore me. This frustrated me further, so I'd accuse him of not loving me. I saw Steve as unemotional, cold, and indifferent; he viewed me as overly sensitive and defensive.

You might be wondering how, thirty-three years later, we have managed to stay together. We've always had two underlying beliefs: we are married for life, and we are going to have a great marriage, even if it kills us (and sometimes I thought it would!).

Wanting to improve my marriage, I read both secular

and Christian books on relationships, love, and communication. Steve wasn't a reader, but he was interested in hearing about what I read. I attended Bible studies and talked with women who had been married longer and whose marriages seemed healthy. I prayed constantly for Steve, our relationship, and my spiritual growth.

Also critical to the durability of our marriage were the people who came alongside us to provide encouragement, insight, and support. Some of the relationships were formal; others, informal. As a young wife, I had the opportunity to share my frustrations about my marriage with a friend named Kathy, who had been married for several years. At first she would call every now and then to chat. As our friendship grew, our conversations became more frequent. Kathy's husband, Gary, traveled with his work like Steve did. She shared that for many years she had bottled up her anger and resentment at his long absences, until she developed an ulcer.

Sometimes Kathy offered me advice; others times she just listened. She pointed me to Scripture passages and encouraged me to grow in my spiritual life. Kathy was an "ear" for my frustrations, but not a "crutch" on which I could lean. When I was at fault in a situation, she pointed that out to me. She was a guide who helped me understand better how to love my husband.

From those rocky early years of our marriage to our current experience of fulfillment and intimacy, Steve and I have come a long way. We are so grateful for the seasoned veterans of married life who took the time to help us, encourage us, and instruct us.

Indeed, that's the way it should be. Titus 2:4 admonishes older women to *teach* the younger women to love their husbands. The implication is that loving your husband doesn't necessarily come naturally; it's a learned skill. And the best way for women to learn is from other women — wives who have "been there, done that" and can pass down their accumulated wisdom and experiences. God, in His infinite wisdom, knew that while Scripture depicts biblical love and provides examples of it, women need a warm-blooded person to come alongside us to help us in our struggles.

In the pages that follow, I want to pass along some of the lessons of love that I've learned in thirty-three years of marriage. I don't claim to be an expert on marital issues, but I have seen my own marriage go from floundering to flourishing over the years. I've learned some things — often the hard way — that I'm happy to share with you. So brew another cup of coffee, settle into your favorite chair, and let's explore together this thing called love.

Love: The World's View Versus God's View

What is love? What does it mean to love someone else?

These are hard questions to begin with, and they're further complicated by a culture that would have us believe love is all about feelings and emotions. Movies, television, music, and books depict the love between a man and a woman as uncontrolled physical passion. The world says such love is "bigger than both of us," a force that carries us away. We're told that we "fall in love," which we can't control. Therefore, we can also "fall out of love," and that's just the way it is. So if a marriage ends, it's nobody's fault.

God's Word, of course, has much to say about love, and Scripture gives a very different picture of love than what we're force-fed by society. Consider two of the Bible's recurring themes:

1. *Love is sacrificial.* The greatest example of love is God sacrificing His Son, Jesus Christ, that we might have

our sins forgiven and our lives redeemed.

2. *Love is unconditional.* This kind of love is not based on performance, and it does not diminish *when* we fail. Romans 8 tells us that nothing can separate us from the love of Christ. As Christ loves us unconditionally, so husbands and wives should love each other. Love should not waver or weaken when our partner fails to meet our expectations.

Loving sacrificially and unconditionally might be totally new concepts to you. In fact, you might think sacrificial, no-strings-attached love is impossible. No human can attain it, right? Not true. As believers in Christ, we have the Holy Spirit within us. When we allow the Spirit to empower us, we are capable of loving our husbands with the love of Christ — sacrificially and unconditionally.

Author Karen Burton Mains speaks of this kind of love:

> A wife is God's gift — a rare and precious offering to her husband. She conveys the Lord's love and care for that man. In this day of pressure, demand and expectation, we need to realize that marriage is more than just one human living with another. It's something sacred. I bring a bit of God into my husband's life. This elevates me from my position as family-car controller, chore keeper and laundry sorter. I am something holy, given to a specific man — my husband.

Debunking the Myths of Love

To understand what it means to love our husbands sacrificially and unconditionally, we must consider what love is and isn't. Let's look at three common myths and their reality checks.

Myth: Love is all about feelings.
Reality: Love is all about commitment and action.

We all know that feelings fluctuate (as do a woman's moods!). If we loved according to our feelings, we would ride a constant emotional roller coaster. Loving by our actions means we *show* love even when we do not necessarily *feel* love. Love acted out is steady and consistent.

According to God's plan, we honor our vows through good and bad times. We do not enter into marriage with the idea that it is anything less than permanent. We don't "jump ship" when marital storms threaten to sink our vessel. Hanging on for dear life, we pull on the life preservers of godly counsel to help us survive.

Learning to love can take time. Being married does not mean we will always be happy. God is not as concerned about our happiness as He is about our obedience to His Word, which includes fulfilling our marriage vows to stick by our spouses through good times and bad.

Myth: For two people meant to be together, love will
come naturally and easily.
Reality: Even under the best of circumstances, love
takes work.

Because true love is based on action and commitment, it doesn't flourish by itself. Love will not automatically increase in amount and intensity as the days and years pass. Spouses must work hard to understand each other, resolve problems, and learn to communicate. This concerted effort will keep love alive and growing through the years.

When Steve and I married, I thought he should *know* how to love me, just as I should know how to love him. One time he said to me, "Tell me what to do to show that I love you, and I'll do it." Not long after that statement, I read a short book entitled *How Do I Say, "I Love You"?* by Judson Swihart. The premise of the book is that certain actions (helping with tasks, touching, listening) demonstrate love, but men and women often have different preferences. After explaining the various actions, the author concludes with a test to determine the top three actions you each prefer. That test was an eye opener for Steve and me! Once we learned the three most important actions each listed, we made an effort to focus on them.

The point is that love—at least the *expression* of love—is something we have to learn and work at.

> *Myth:* Love means everything in marriage will be fifty-fifty and totally equal.
>
> *Reality:* Love means giving 100 percent, even when it feels unfair.

Throw out your scorecard and forget the idea that your husband should meet you halfway in everything. Married love means giving 100 percent regardless of what your husband is giving. Sound unfair? From our human perspective, it is. But remember: "While we were still sinners, Christ died for us" (Romans 5:8). He gave His all, though we deserved nothing. We can't do less in loving our mate.

Forgetting the fifty-fifty idea of the world's view, we must love as we know God wants us to. James 4:17 states, "Anyone, then, who knows the good he ought to do and doesn't do it, sins." This has been a key verse for me whenever I've wanted to give in to feelings of unfairness. We are not to keep a tally of who's expressing love better or more often. As Christ said, we must forgive seventy-seven times (Matthew 18:21-22). We must forgive and love over and over, even when our husbands seem to be making no effort to do the same. Will this be easy? No. Will we ever tire of being the "giver"? Yes. Will we sometimes want to throw in the towel? Probably. We are human.

However, the closer our relationship to God, the easier it will be to love unconditionally and sacrificially. We can love our mates with a biblical love only with the power of the Holy Spirit. Therefore, it is important to maintain a close bond with the Lord so He can empower us to love our husbands in the way He intends.

Let's Get Practical: The Specifics of Love and How to Express It

The biblical pattern of Christian love is spelled out in 1 Corinthians 13. While this passage refers to *all* relationships, marriage is perhaps the best—and most difficult—context in which to live out this godly love. We can apply the elements of love in verses 4 through 8 to the husband-wife relationship in some practical ways:

- ◆ Love is patient. It forgives a husband's annoying habits or preoccupation with work.
- ◆ Love is kind. It doesn't nag or complain when his job requires extra time or travel.
- ◆ Love does not envy. It rejoices at his job promotion or special recognition.
- ◆ Love does not boast. It doesn't brag about being better at something or earning a higher salary than he does.
- ◆ Love is not proud. It readily gives him credit for his ideas and suggestions.
- ◆ Love is not rude. It never puts him down in front of his children or other people.
- ◆ Love is not self-seeking. It gladly allows him time to pursue his hobby or play golf with friends.
- ◆ Love is not easily angered. It is long-suffering and does not retaliate for his anger.

◆ Love keeps no record of wrongs. It forgives mistakes and forgets past wrongs.

◆ Love does not delight in evil. It does not ask him to do something wrong.

◆ Love rejoices with the truth. It offers praise when he seeks to understand himself more clearly.

◆ Love always protects. It stands by his side in support of his leadership.

◆ Love always trusts. It believes the best about him and gives him the benefit of the doubt.

◆ Love always hopes. It encourages him when his job is changed or phased out.

◆ Love always perseveres. It stays committed regardless of the stresses and storms of life.

◆ Love never fails. It remains steadfast even though youth and health might fade.

Keeping in mind the previous list, let's look at a few specific ways to cultivate love in your marriage.

1. *Study your husband.* Make a list of his strengths, another of his weaknesses. Tear the list of weaknesses into little pieces and throw them away. Review the list of strengths each day. Focus on a particular strength for a week, and ask God to make you aware of it in your husband. Concentrating on his positive attributes will kindle appreciation for him and help keep you from finding fault with him. Give him one sincere compliment each day. Remember, your husband is an imperfect person and you must accept him as he is.

2. *Listen to him.* Many women (especially those with young children) are excellent at "multi-tasking"—doing several things simultaneously, including carrying on a conversation while working. But to demonstrate your interest in what your husband says, stop what you are doing and focus on him. Make good eye contact. Ask questions.

Encourage him to tell you more. After all, few things convey love and honor more than active listening.

3. *Commit to a mutually fulfilling sexual relationship.* Learn what your husband enjoys, communicate your desires, and make time to be alone together. (Not always an easy feat with children in the house!) Be creative. Be daring. Most husbands love to have their wives initiate sexual intimacy.

Above all else, be willing to change yourself. As you improve, so will he!

How to Love Your Husband If You're Not on the Same Spiritual Wavelength

Perhaps you and your husband married when you were both unbelievers, and you later came to faith in God—but he didn't. Or maybe you were a Christian who went ahead and married a nonbeliever because you were ambivalent about your faith at the time. Whatever the case, now you find yourself "unequally yoked" with your spouse.

Fortunately, this is an issue that's clearly and specifically addressed in Scripture. Paul writes in Corinthians that you should remain with an unbelieving husband unless he chooses to leave. But how can you love him sacrificially and unconditionally when you're on a different wavelength?

Three things are most important in this situation:

1. *Pray for your husband.* Pray every day that God would bring people and events into his life that will open his heart to the gospel. Some wives have prayed for their husbands for decades and finally—after most people would have given up hope—the man accepts Christ as Savior. Keep praying and never, ever give up.

2. *Win him over with God's love.* With the Spirit's help,

model joy, peace, and trust. Perhaps through your example, your husband will come to know and accept Christ.

3. *Find an older woman who's been there.* Seek out someone in your church or Christian women's group who has been in the same situation. She can give you insights and suggestions for loving your unbelieving husband. Don't be afraid to ask for help. An older woman will feel honored to assist and advise you.

A far more common issue women wrestle with is being more spiritually mature than their spouse. Women seem more willing than men to take advantage of Bible study groups, Christian books and tapes, and conferences and seminars, which help them mature spiritually. Perhaps their desire for close relationships and intimacy plays a part in their desire for spiritual growth.

Men, on the other hand, are generally not as ready to pursue opportunities for spiritual growth. Some men don't feel comfortable meeting with other men in small groups. In recent years, Promise Keepers has provided the opportunity for men to be challenged, inspired, and motivated to become the spiritual leaders of their families. The large numbers of men who have been involved in Promise Keepers rallies and events like Stand in the Gap demonstrate that men are hungry for spiritual meaning in their lives. However, once the excitement of the event has worn off, many men revert to their old habits. Some men participate in small groups to nurture their spiritual life and be accountable to one another, but many (perhaps most) men insist they don't have the time or the need for such groups.

God is aware of this situation. He will mature you both in His time and at the speed at which you allow. If your growth occurs faster, that's okay. Never let your concern for who grows more hold you back from spiritual activities. You do what God leads you to do, and leave your husband to God. It's not your responsibility to grow up your husband spiritually, but to love him unconditionally.

At this point, you may be able to share with him what you are learning in a non-threatening, non-preaching, non-accusatory way. You might tell him about what you read or offer him tapes that you have enjoyed. You can gently encourage him to attend men's activities. Your attitude will be the key. It's important and wise not to become judgmental or critical of your husband. If you accept him as he is, love him, support him, and encourage him in all aspects of his life, he might be receptive to your suggestions. You might join a couples' study group or attend a seminar together. Most of all, you can pray for his growth. Still, it bears repeating: you are not your husband's spiritual leader; God is.

When Love Fades

Over time, we can unconsciously take our husband and marriage for granted. We don't pay as much attention to cultivating our relationship as we once did. We become comfortable in our marriage, or we unwittingly develop individual lives.

There are periods of time when Steve's work takes him away from home. I have learned to fill the time when he's away so the days don't seem too long or lonely. The down side is that we could easily begin to lead separate lives. We recognized this danger early in our marriage, so we have always planned special times together to reconnect when Steve returns. Steve also calls me every night he's away. He started this practice when our kids were young, so he could talk with each one and keep up on their activities. Now there's only me at home, but he still calls.

There are highs and lows in all marriages. Expect

them. Not every morning will you wake up madly in love with your man. (Some mornings just waking up is tough!) Unfortunately, many people head to divorce court when love fades. Maybe you haven't taken such a drastic step, but you believe you no longer love your husband. If so, pray about your feelings. Be honest with God. Ask Him to help you rediscover your love.

Think about why you were first attracted to him. Remember how that early love felt. Try some of the ideas mentioned in this chapter. And be patient—love doesn't fade in a day and neither will it be revived quickly. If you continue to develop your walk with God, obey His Word, and love your husband with your actions, the feelings will ultimately follow.

DIGGING DEEPER

1. Name some differences between the world's view of love and God's view. Which view would you say you have been focusing on in your marriage?

2. Which "myth of love" mentioned in this chapter has influenced you the most? How?

3. What are some actions that can help you focus on the needs of your mate instead of yourself?

4. Why is it important that the older women teach the younger about marriage, especially in today's world?

5. How is your relationship with God crucial to loving your husband?

6. What command are we given in 1 John 3:11, 1 John 4:7, and 2 John 1:5?

7. What important truth about love do we learn from 1 John 3:18?

8. Which of the ideas listed in the "Let's Get Practical" section do you do well? Which could you improve on?

9. Read John 15:1-17 and answer the following questions.
   a. What type of relationship between God and those who believe in Him is depicted in these verses?

   b. What commands does He give you?

   c. What promises will be yours?

10. What hope is offered in the verses below?
    2 Corinthians 12:9

    2 Corinthians 9:8

11. How can we awaken "faded" love?

12. Why will you be able to love your husband as God
    intends?

Chapter Three

A Heritage from the Lord

Loving Your Children

By Janet Cox

Then [the older women] can train the younger
women to love their . . . children.

Titus 2:4

Have you ever read *The Velveteen Rabbit,* the story
of a young boy who comes to love his stuffed
rabbit? Near the beginning of the story, the
Rabbit asks the Skin Horse (the wisest and oldest of the
toys in the nursery), "What is Real?"

"Real isn't how you are made," said the Skin
Horse. "It's a thing that happens to you. When a
child loves you for a long time, not just to play
with, but *really* loves, then you become Real."
"Does it hurt?" asked the Rabbit.
"Sometimes," said the Skin Horse, for he was

always truthful. "When you are Real, you don't mind being hurt."

"Does it happen all at once, like being wound up," he asked, "or bit by bit?"

"It doesn't happen all at once," said the Skin Horse. "You become. It takes a long time."[1]

This snippet of dialogue says so much about loving someone; and it can be applied to a mother's love, a love that is unselfish and giving. While a child's love grows "bit by bit," a mother's love grows in leaps and bounds day by day, and at times it does hurt to love our children. Once a mother holds her child in her arms, her whole life is changed as she loves, nurtures, and encourages her boy or girl to become all God wants him or her to be. That is part of becoming real!

Those eight words in Titus 2:4 that form the command regarding our offspring—"train the younger women to love their . . . children"—look deceptively simple and innocent at first glance. But if you have children, you know how challenging and frustrating the task of child rearing can be. If you don't have children, you've probably heard friends with kids talk about the enormous joys and struggles of parenthood. Believe them!

As if raising children in today's dangerous and bewildering culture is not formidable enough, *Christian* mothers have an even greater responsibility. We are to nurture our children's *souls* as well as their bodies and minds. We must teach our young ones to love and honor God, which is not an easy task. Matthew Henry, in his classic commentary on the Bible, tells us to love our children "not with a natural affection only, but a spiritual love, a love springing from a holy sanctified heart and regulated by the Word."[2]

In an interview, singer-songwriter Amy Grant once told how God put a thought in her mind regarding her expected son: this child will someday be a fellow-laborer with you in God's kingdom. That picture awed her. Almost every woman who has borne a child loves him or her to the best of her ability; but with Christ's love in our hearts, we are able to love and nourish them in body, soul, and spirit to a greater dimension. I find that exciting!

This is precisely why the Titus 2 passage is so wise: Young mothers *need* the wisdom of those who have "been there." And that is the spirit in which I write this chapter.

Our Children: A Kaleidoscope

As I sat in my study reflecting on the importance of nurturing our children, I noticed a kaleidoscope that sits on my bookcase. What a fascinating and delightful experience it is to bring the kaleidoscope to your eye and turn it to see the many different images that emerge.

The word *kaleidoscope* means "beautiful form," and that is indeed what blossoms forth before the eye. The tube contains mirrors and pieces of colored glass, paper, or plastic. The reflections of these "nuggets" produce changing patterns when the tube is rotated. The pattern is the result of simple objects placed in the end of the tube, but the combination of these objects presents a rare and complex picture with many unique images. So it is with our children. There is a great simplicity as well as an unlimited complexity to them. As we love our children, the results can be as intricate as a kaleidoscope image.

Let's look at five nuggets you can put into the kaleidoscope of your children's lives that will contribute to the mosaic of the person each will become.

Nugget #1: Quality and Quantity Time
Suppose you were asked, "In what concrete ways do you know that someone loves you?" Your answer would

probably be something like, "He takes the time to listen to me." Or, "She was there for me when I needed a friend." For any relationship, time is the critical element for expressing love.

In his book *How to Really Love Your Children,* Dr. Ross Campbell offers three simple techniques that convey value to your child: eye contact, physical contact, and focused attention. He says, "They work like this: When you have something positive to say to your child, get down on his level, put your hand on his shoulder, look straight into his eyes, then give him your words of love."[3] Campbell goes on to say that parents often use physical contact and eye contact only when scolding their children. When our children have something to say to us, we should stop and focus on them and really listen. This takes time.

Sometimes life gets so hectic that Mom can't do it all. We become so consumed with life's hassles and headaches, problems and pressures that we forget to take time with our kids. To make sure I focused on my kids when they were young, I would have a "Love Joel Day" or a "Love Christopher Day." For instance, when I knew Christopher was struggling—when he was having a rough time at school or when his asthma made it hard to breathe—I would enlist the rest of the family to give extra hugs and affirmation to him. I would spend extra time reading to him or playing games, and I'd make his favorite meal for dinner. This attention and encouragement showed Christopher that we were all working together.

Taking time to maintain a routine in the home is another way to demonstrate love. Some children need this structure more than others do. Knowing when it is time for meals, bed, play, school, and other activities provides emotional security. However, be careful that lists and schedules do not start to control you.

I remember going through periods of being so busy

doing things according to my schedule that I sacrificed quality time with my children. It would show up in their behavior! They would whine, fuss, and squabble with one another. The Holy Spirit would check me as to what was more important: accomplishing the tasks on my "to do" list or having happy children. I would then take a day or two and concentrate more on them. There are many ways to love these precious ones, but all take time!

NUGGET #2: CONSISTENT DISCIPLINE

Another nugget we can place into the kaleidoscope of our children's lives is *discipline*. One dictionary defines discipline as bringing under control by training and obedience. What's more, the book of Proverbs has several verses that give direct and applicable thoughts on child discipline:

- ◆ Train a child in the way he should go, and when he is old he will not turn from it. (22:6)
- ◆ Folly is bound up in the heart of a child, but the rod of discipline will drive it far from him. (22:15)
- ◆ The rod of correction imparts wisdom, but a child left to himself disgraces his mother. (29:15)

These verses remind us of the importance of providing the direction a child needs. However, a word of caution is given to us in Ephesians 6:4: "Fathers, do not exasperate your children; instead, bring them up in the training and instruction of the Lord." Of course, this advice also applies to mothers. Don't punish unfairly, and make sure discipline is appropriate for the misbehavior. Each child is unique and the method of discipline might be different for each one. For one child, you can just give him "the look" when he's done something wrong, and he'll burst into tears. Another may require a stronger form of discipline.

Larry Christenson, a noted Christian author, writes,

"Discipline is the other side of teaching. A child with a teachable spirit will still need thorough explanation, much patience, opportunity to try and experiment, including the right to fail and learn by failure." He goes on to say that a willful, disobedient, or rebellious child is not teachable, and God expects us to give firm and loving discipline. The Bible does not condone physical abuse, though correction may be painful at times. We need to remember that a child's eternal destiny may hinge upon godly discipline provided by parents.[4]

NUGGET #3: SET A GOOD EXAMPLE

Being a role model is a critical part of training children. Paul instructed Timothy: "Set an example . . . in speech, in life, in love, in faith and in purity" (1 Timothy 4:12). In other words, conduct yourself so that your life is an excellent example of Christlike living. Other than God Himself, no one knows us better than our children do. We need to stop occasionally and consider what kind of example our lives project.

Think of the times you have seen a young son follow as his father mows the yard, or a little daughter caring for a doll as her mother cares for a baby. Being a good spiritual role model for our children is critical! Grow in your walk with Jesus in order to impart the greatness of God's love. Do you find it hard to squeeze in time for Bible reading and prayer? This is a common problem for moms with young children. Keep your Bible—along with a devotional such as *Our Daily Bread* and a notepad—in a convenient place. Ask God to help you find a fifteen-minute block of time to spend with Him. You might have a rough start, but He is faithful. You very well might be interrupted, but seeing Mom reading her Bible or down on her knees in prayer will be a lasting example to your children. This can also open doors for many good conversations about spiritual matters.

Dr. James Dobson, author and president of Focus on the Family, expresses the importance of providing a good example in spiritual matters:

> In no sense should we be casual or neutral about the spiritual training of our children. Their world should sparkle with references to Jesus and to our faith. Talking about spiritual things should not be reserved just for Sunday or for a bedtime prayer. Rather it should characterize our conversation and be part of the fabric of our lives.
>
> Why? Because our children are watching our every move during those early years. They want to know what is most important to us. If we hope to instill within them a faith that will last for a lifetime, then they must see and feel our passion for God.[5]

In addition to teaching them to read the Bible and pray through our example, Dobson suggests the following two verses to evaluate whether your child is growing spiritually.

1. *"Love the Lord your God with all your heart and with all your soul and with all your mind and with all your strength"* (Mark 12:30). This verse points them to God. Is your child learning:

◆ The love of God through the love, tenderness, and mercy he sees in you?
◆ To talk about the Lord and include Him in his thoughts and plans?
◆ To trust Jesus for help whenever he is frightened, anxious, or lonely?
◆ The meaning of faith, trust, and joy, and of Jesus' birth and death?

2. *"Love your neighbor as yourself"* (Mark 12:31). This verse focuses on their relationship with others. Is your child learning:

- ◆ To understand and empathize with the feelings of others?
- ◆ To share and not to be selfish or demanding?
- ◆ Not to gossip and criticize others?
- ◆ To grow in self-confidence?[6]

These are only two Bible verses, but if we apply these admonitions to our lives and pass them on to our children, their lives will be changed—for eternity. The old adage "Actions speak louder than words" is definitely true for children. Are your actions and attitude providing a godly example for your children?

NUGGET #4: INSTRUCTION IN GOD'S WORD
The instructions in Deuteronomy 6:7 tell us to teach our children about God whenever we have opportunity: "Impress [God's commandments] on your children. Talk about them when you sit at home and when you walk along the road, when you lie down and when you get up." Let's look at a few of the key phrases:

- ◆ *When you walk along the road.* This brings to my mind not just walking, but also all that time we spend in the car and even vacation times when the tempo of our life might be a little more relaxed.
- ◆ *When you lie down.* This means talking to your children about God and telling them Bible stories at bedtime or before naps.
- ◆ *When you rise up.* Naturally, the intention here is to start your day with God. Every morning, pray

for God's guidance and invite Him to be your constant companion throughout the day.

My husband, Allen, and I found it natural to teach our children the name of Jesus. We were given a picture of Christ as a wedding gift, and we hung it in our bedroom above our bed. When the children reached the age where they could climb out of their beds and into ours, we would lie there and engage them in conversation. One of the first words we taught them was *Jesus* as we pointed to the picture on the wall. This brought Him into their awareness at an early age.

Another way to nurture your children's spiritual life is to teach them Bible verses as soon as they can make sentences. Between the ages of eighteen and twenty-four months, a child's mind is like a sponge. Children parrot just about everything they hear and see. Why not use this for their spiritual advantage? Teach them John 3:16 and other verses. Begin the habit of taking them to Sunday school. As they grow, take them to programs at your local church. Vacation Bible School in the summer and the Awana program during the school year are excellent ways to learn biblical principles.

NUGGET #5: TEACH THEM THE POWER OF PRAYER

Some parents make bedtime prayers a priority. In our home, we prayed together at the evening meal. We could pray for anything that was of concern to any of us — friends, family, school, sickness, and upcoming decisions. We also joined in thanks for answered prayers. In this way, mealtime was closely associated with prayer time.

Once when our family was traveling on vacation, we stopped at a busy restaurant for breakfast. There were six of us and the hostess sat us at a large table in an area that was elevated, three steps up from the other tables. As the waitress brought our breakfast, our four-year-old said loudly, "Don't forget to pray!" Everyone in the restaurant heard him and some smiled. Needless to say, we prayed, even as many restaurant patrons looked on.

Prayer is, indeed, a pivotal part of spiritual training for children — and their parents. I learned a lesson about praying for "insignificant" things when our oldest son was six years old. We had a large plot in a community garden and went there each weekend to garden. There was a weedy patch next to it where our three boys would run and play while Allen and I hoed and planted.

One day while working I heard a desperate cry across the tops of tall weeds: "Mom, I can't find my pocket knife! I lost my knife!"

This was a special knife given to my son Joel by a well-liked uncle. The fact that it couldn't cut hot butter didn't matter. It was a coming-of-age thing; he was old enough to carry this pearl-handled knife in his pocket like a man.

"Are you sure it's not in your pocket?" I calmly replied.

It wasn't, so we all joined in to search for it. But there was no sign of the knife where they had been playing.

Then Joel's younger brother, Chris, piped up: "Let's ask Jesus to help us find it."

I thought, *Uh-oh, this will really be an exercise in faith. It'll be impossible to find that knife in these tall weeds!* At the same time, I wanted my kids to know the reality of answered prayer.

So the four children gathered around me and I prayed, "Jesus, help us find Joel's knife. You know where it is, so now please show us where it is."

I don't think I have ever prayed a prayer with less faith. However, our God is faithful. We went searching again, and a few moments later, Joel shouted from a corner of the patch, "Look! Here's my knife!"

There was the lost pocket knife, lying in a little open space. He knew God had led him to it, and that was a lesson in faith for us all. God had answered that prayer according to the children's trust, not mine. It's true that God makes up for what parents lack in many ways.

Looking Forward

As mothers, we are sculptors of our children's lives, and many times it seems our efforts are not producing the brilliant results that we see in our friends' or neighbors' children. That doesn't mean we are not being successful. I came across a poem the other day that Joel wrote when he was ten. It still serves as a reminder to me that success is not the same for everyone.

SUCCESS

Success is a perfect math paper
Success is a hard job done
Success is a straight "A" report card
Success is a victory won.

Success is helping a little child
Success is winning a game
Success is throwing a touchdown pass
Success is never the same.[7]

Success is never the same. There are a variety of ways a mother can fulfill her God-given role. The many nuggets we place into the kaleidoscope of our children's lives will yield different results for each—and the end result is not in our hands, but His.

A few years ago, my husband and I celebrated our thirtieth wedding anniversary. My husband did not want an "open house" gathering. So our children, being creative types, came up with a great alternative, one we'll remember for a lifetime. It featured them playing and singing our favorite songs, some together and some solo. One of the best parts was a poem written by our daughter, Angela, and put to music by Joel. The following is a portion of the song that showed how our actions impacted their lives.

TOGETHER

We had Santa Claus at Christmas,
But we had Jesus all year long,
A mom and dad together,
A precious faith,
And a place where we belonged,
And no idea of how much we really had.

There were seasons of plenty and seasons of need
Sometimes we thought the strikes would last forever.
But a simple lack of money cannot sever bonds of
      faith.
A little hope, a lot of prayer,
The blessings poured in from everywhere!
We saw the smile of Dad and Mom
And felt our own convictions growing strong.[8]

We cannot know what all of those nuggets of time, love, discipline, teaching, prayer, and instruction in God's Word will yield. But we have the assurance that He who promised is faithful. Remain faithful to Him, and one day you will see birthed in the kaleidoscope of your child's life a picture with colors more beautiful than a rainbow and shapes more complex than the works of an artist!

DIGGING DEEPER

1. Besides the five suggested in this chapter, what other "nuggets" are you putting into the kaleidoscope of your children's lives?

2. Read 1 Corinthians 13:1-7 and list five definitions of love that are important for mothers to remember.
   a.

   b.

   c.

   d.

   e.

3. How do discipline and instruction demonstrate love to our children, according to these verses:
Proverbs 13:24

Proverbs 20:11

Proverbs 22:6,15

Proverbs 29:15

4. How does discipline differ from punishment?

5. Read Deuteronomy 6:4-9 and answer the following questions.

How are we instructed to love the Lord our God?
a.

b.

c.

What are we to do with these commandments?

When are we to teach our children God's Word?
a.

b.

c.

6. Paul prayed for his spiritual children in the passages listed below. What can you take from these prayers to apply to your own children?
Ephesians 1:17-19

Philippians 1:9-11

Colossians 1:9-12

7. What Christian values are most important for you to pass down to your children?

Chapter Four

WHO'S IN CONTROL HERE?

Self-Control and Temptation

BY ANGIE CONRAD

Then [the older women] can train the younger
women to . . . be self-controlled.

Titus 2:4-5

T he battle lines are drawn. On one side are the
heavyweight issues: addiction, promiscuity, being
critical, food compulsions, jealousy, adultery,
lying, image, and fear. On the other side is one little, right-
eous virtue called self-control.

How can you and I withstand powerful temptations
and problems armed only with self-control? Doesn't seem
like a fair fight, does it? Sounds like Goliath on one side
and the youngster David on the other.

In chapters 2 and 3, you read and studied about emotionally supporting and loving your husband and children.
You might now be holding your breath, thinking, *Not only*

do I have to take care of my family, but now you're telling me I must learn to control myself with sheer willpower!

It is a bit overwhelming, isn't it?

I know my first thought about writing a chapter on self-control was, *Who me?* Considering myself lacking in this virtue, I found it ironic that God would want to use me to help others explore how to be self-controlled. I constantly struggle with many of the issues on the losing side of the battle line and have spent a good portion of my forty-five years trying to track down what seems to be an illusion to me—self-control.

So, what's the big deal, anyway? Because we are all in the same boat, no one holds our lack of self-control against us, right? You might ask yourself:

◆ Isn't just about every role model in Hollywood dealing with an addiction?
◆ What's wrong with a six-pack after a long, hard work week?
◆ Doesn't everyone binge on food sometimes? After all, food is *so* good.
◆ In most cases, isn't being critical just telling the truth?
◆ Bad things happen all the time; isn't it normal to be fearful?

We fool ourselves into believing that lack of self-control is normal. The truth is, the lack of self-control causes the biggest problems in our lives today.

What Is Self-Control, Anyway?

Let's be honest. Self-control is not a popular concept in our culture. Aside from the occasional sermon on the topic, we don't hear much about controlling our actions and attitudes. So we'd better start by defining our terms. *The American Heritage Dictionary* defines self-control as "control of one's emotions, desires, or actions by one's own will." Interestingly, the Bible describes it in a totally different way. The apostle Paul tells us in Galatians 5:22-23: "But the fruit [result] of the Spirit [through a personal relationship with Christ] is love, joy, peace, patience, kindness, goodness, faithfulness, gentleness and self-control."

Can you see the difference between these two explanations? The dictionary's definition implies, "It's all up to you. You must do it on your own." The Bible, on the other hand, tells us that through fellowship and faith in Jesus, the Holy Spirit is there to help us. And what better help can we get than the Spirit of God, along with His instruction in the Bible.

So why do we as Christians constantly find ourselves doing things we know are more harmful than helpful to us? And why do we often feel powerless to resist? Our will to resist temptations is overwhelmed by the compulsion to not be left out of what appears to be fun. We believe our participation will feel good *temporarily* even though we know the results may cause us to feel bad *indefinitely*. Our self-destructive proclivities strip us of self-control. We only have to look at Adam and Eve to see that humans tend to be swayed by self-destructive emotions rather than sound reasoning. We all seem to have blind spots when it comes to making healthy, God-honoring decisions.

Perhaps you have already learned through your own painful failures that doing anything without the help of God sets you up for even more painful consequences and huge disappointments. I know I am still dealing with the not-so-fun consequences of my ungodly early adulthood.

In the following pages, we will examine some common pitfalls and factors that hinder us from developing self-control.

TEMPTATIONS

In many Christian circles, the mention of sexual temptation and immorality and their consequences tends to be swept under the proverbial rug. We prefer to hide this kind of dirt from the outside world. Unfortunately, we cannot ignore the power of sexual temptation just because it makes us uncomfortable to publicly confront it. You might find the prevalent reports of sexual misconduct in marriage shocking, but in reality, it does happen in Christian marriages. And it doesn't do any good to ignore and deny it. Let's take a look at two people in the Bible who struggled with self-control in this tantalizing arena of temptation.

Joseph was the guy with the colorful coat, the favorite son of Jacob, and the much-hated, pain-in-the-neck brother of Jacob's other offspring. After Joseph was sold into slavery by his brothers, he found himself as the right-hand man of Potiphar, one of Pharaoh's most important officials. Throughout the biblical account of Joseph, we see that the Lord was with Joseph and that Joseph gave the Lord credit for all of his successes (see Genesis 37–50). When Potiphar's wife tried to seduce Joseph, he was able to resist. He determined that he would not sin against God or Potiphar. He controlled his emotions, not willing to have a moment of lust destroy his relationship with God.

Contrast Joseph with another Old Testament icon, Samson (read about him in the book of Judges). He, too, was set aside at birth by God, who had great plans for him. But when Samson was put under similar sexual pressures, he succumbed to temptation. What was the difference? When Samson insisted on having a Philistine wife—one forbidden by God—he was led by emotions. He saw something he wanted, and he went after it. Of course, he suffered the consequences when his wife manipulated and betrayed him.

We see Samson dig another, deeper hole through his

relationship with Delilah. The excitement of a challenge and its immediate rewards—as well as the delayed punishment—helped Samson feel powerful and competent. This happens to us as well. How ironic that the lack of self-control initially makes us feel in control! And once we give in to temptation, it stealthily strengthens our desire to do it again. Once we let go of our control over our emotions, it becomes harder to rein them in the next time we are tempted. Joseph reined in his emotional desires; Samson did not.

Another unfortunate example of sexual temptation comes from a friend of mine, whom I'll call Abby. What started as counseling sessions with her minister evolved into flirtation . . . then an inappropriately close friendship . . . then a full-blown affair. Their physical and emotional relationship ended up careening out of control and causing such a collision that, four years later, the parts of her marriage are still being welded together.

"Every day I live with the regret and pain of succumbing to temptation," Abby told me. "I destroyed the faith and trust of my spouse and family with reckless acts and now live with their hurt and suspicion as we rebuild our relationships." As painful as the results have been, Abby feels blessed because many times a collision like this "totals" a marriage beyond salvage. Abby and her husband, Doug, are committed to rebuilding their relationship.

I asked Abby what she could have done to avoid this near-fatal "fiery crash." Here, in essence, is what she said:

Go to God. "When I was weak, I didn't go to God," she admitted. "I knew He would say 'stop,' so I avoided Him and rationalized my actions. I clearly let Satan have the upper hand." Abby paraphrased Hebrews 4:16: "Go to God boldly because He will help you in time of need."

Recognize your vulnerabilities. Search your past to discover if you are susceptible to a particular area of temptation.

You may have had a traumatic experience that unconsciously weakens your confidence and self-control. Abby found this to be her case after further counseling.

Confide in your spouse. "I loved my husband and still do," Abby said. "If I had only confided in him at the first sign of inappropriate behavior from our minister, Doug could have and would have been a shield of protection and a defense mechanism. We would have been fighting this temptation with the strength of two."

Flee, flee, flee. As difficult as it may be, you must turn and run when temptation presents itself. Remove yourself completely from the person or addiction pulling you like a magnet. Only God can give you this strength. Make every temptation an occasion to trust God.

Confide in a "safe" person. Talk to a friend who will honor your confidence, but who will also talk honestly and forcefully with you. Verbally confiding in someone you trust provides accountability and helps you make rational, not emotional, decisions.

We talked about the results of the affair that continue to affect Abby and Doug's marriage. "Communication has to be reconstructed," she told me. "I now know that personal sin affects other people; it is not isolated to me. Adultery destroyed Doug's trust in me and the security of my children. Some days, an atmosphere of pain, hurt, and suspicion hangs like a cloud waiting to rain on my life."

Abby admitted she must be "on guard" at all times and take care of any "chinks in her armor" immediately. "I realize that one small action can grow into much larger temptation issues," she said.

In the midst of all the dark clouds surrounding Abby, there is a ray of sunlight breaking through—God's grace. "I am experiencing God's love and forgiveness as I come to better understand Christ's atonement for our sins," she said. "Accepting God's grace is not something that happens all at once. It has been a process as I've owned up to my failings and grasped the fact that Jesus' sacrifice covers *all* our terrible deeds."

BEING CRITICAL

Even though we are all "in the same battle" when it comes to self-control issues, we usually end up trying to put ourselves above the fray. We might say something like, "I would never steal office supplies from my company!" No, but we might rob a coworker of her reputation by spreading a nasty rumor.

Often we rationalize our own lack of self-control even as we criticize others. Conversations like the following—which occur more often than we'd like to admit—remind us that criticism, fault-finding, and rumor-mongering are temptations run amok:

> "Mary's darling little children would be more tolerable if she would be more assertive with her discipline."
>
> "That's true, but not only that—and you didn't hear it from me—Mary's husband is fooling around with his secretary."
>
> "You're kidding! Poor Mary."
>
> "Of course, if Mary took a little more care with her appearance, she might be able to keep her husband home."
>
> "Maybe, but her home is such a mess, it's no wonder he goes elsewhere!"

Or maybe you're the one who has taken a few well-aimed potshots at others. Many times we use the excuse "I'm just being honest" or "I'm just trying to be helpful." In reality, we are usually trying to build ourselves up at the expense of someone else.

I'll never forget the criticism and judgment that stung me at a difficult time. My second child had just been born, and we were devastated to learn he had the same incurable genetic disease as his older brother, which I wrote of in the Introduction. It was a time of great pain and confusion for my husband and me.

During this time, I found great comfort in our church and particularly in my women's Bible study group. To my dismay, I became aware of a judgmental, critical spirit in that special group. One woman posed the question (behind my back, of course) as to why I would ever be so bold— meaning *stupid*—to have another child when I already had one with a terrible disease. She felt I deserved whatever came my way due to my "lack of common sense." I was devastated to hear that. Not only did I feel betrayed by this "Christian" woman, but I was also inadvertently made aware of how often we judge others without knowing the facts or the hearts of those we criticize.

Are you self-controlled when it comes to judging others? Or are you lacking compassion and self-control? We never paint a pretty picture of ourselves when we are negative and critical of others. We are to have compassion and mercy toward others as Jesus has compassion and mercy toward us. He did not feel the need to build Himself up by criticizing others.

ADDICTIONS

When it comes to addictions such as alcohol, food, drugs, cigarettes, or gambling, we are often in denial. We allow ourselves to dabble in these arenas because they are "socially acceptable." Granted, Scripture does not specifically identify and spell out every last pitfall we should avoid. But God's Word is clear about the dangers of excess and of being a bad example to others.

We rationalize our excessive behavior by saying, "I can

stop anytime I want to." Or, "This is a special occasion." Or perhaps the lamest of all, "Boys will be boys" (and "girls will be girls"). We refuse to believe that we are personally responsible for our behaviors and that self-control takes practice. We usually categorize each of these behaviors and separate ourselves from those who do them. We have the smokers over there, the adulterers over there, the overeaters over there, and the compulsive dieters over there. Pigeonholing other people takes the focus off ourselves and our own issues.

FEAR AND DOUBT

Has this ever happened to you? You are home alone. Maybe you are single or divorced, or your spouse is out of town. During the daylight hours, all is well. You relish the quiet or delight in an unstructured schedule. Life is blissful. But soon night falls . . . and it's really, really dark outside. Fear sinks its gnarly, spindly fingers into you. The grip slowly tightens as you keep telling yourself there is no reason to be afraid. But you don't believe it!

You double-check the doors and windows, turn on the outside lights, peek into the closets, and turn on the television. Still, an ugly, strangling fear doesn't allow you any peace or security. Then it starts. What if, what if, what if . . . ?

Or how about these?

◆ Your pastor asks you to share your testimony in church next Sunday night. "You want *me* to stand up in front of a room full of strangers and tell about my life? But I hate public speaking. No, I just couldn't."

◆ Your boss tells you he's going on a business trip and wants you to run the weekly departmental meeting. "Me?" you say. "You're kidding. What would my coworkers think if I tried to fill the boss's shoes?"

◆ A neighbor asks you to go with her when she serves Thanksgiving dinner at the local soup kitchen. "Well," you respond, "I like the idea of helping the poor, but isn't that in a bad part of town? It just seems a little . . . I don't know, *dangerous.*"

All of these opportunities sound exciting until Mr. Fear and his wife, Mrs. Doubt, sashay into your mind and start rattling chains and pumping up the pressure, taking away your self-control. "AHHHHHHHHH!" you scream. "I can't do this!" Paralyzed by panic and fear, you are unable to pursue these opportunities.

How can we learn to control unbridled fear? As always, God shows us the way. Remember when God told Jeremiah that He had appointed him to be a prophet? Jeremiah's reply to God wasn't one of self-assuredness and self-control. Instead, he said, "I do not know how to speak; I am only a child" (Jeremiah 1:6). In other words, "No way, Lord. You have the wrong guy here." God assured Jeremiah that He indeed had the right person: "Do not be afraid . . . for I am with you and will rescue you" (verse 8). Those are good words to hang our fears on.

Need a little more assurance? Whenever I am afraid about speaking or testifying, I think of Moses in Exodus 4. God tells Moses he has been chosen to lead God's people out of Egypt. Moses is in shock and full of fear. He begs God, "O Lord, *pleeeease* send someone else to do it" (4:13, emphasis added).

I relate. Can you? Moses, the father of the nation of Israel, is whining! So how did God respond? Even though He was perturbed with Moses, He assured him, "Now go; I will help you speak and will teach you what to say"

(4:12). You can take great comfort from that statement. Whenever God is telling you to pursue something difficult, rest assured that He will give you the knowledge and skill to do the job. If we use self-control against our fear and rely on God, He gives the comfort and courage to get the job done.

THE NOT-SO-PERFECT IMAGE

"Do I look all right?" This is a familiar question that rings in the ears of most women. We are concerned about how we measure up when judged against the standards of society. The media has sold us on what constitutes a perfect image. They tell us how we should look, how we should feel, and how we should gauge our success. We hungrily swallow the pictures and advertisements in magazines like *Glamour, People*, and *Cosmopolitan*.

The pressure to conform to the world is powerful. We sit in the beauty shops poring over pictures in search of the right haircuts. We try on hundreds of dresses, searching for just the right one. And we run ourselves ragged trying to decorate our homes, keep them clean, and manicure our lawns. We certainly want to be held in high esteem in our neighborhood.

Not that there is anything wrong with wanting to look and feel good about ourselves and our families. But we tend to go overboard and become *driven* to present a great image. We believe the television and magazine ads when they tell us we are too large or too small or too *whatever*.

You might be dealing with the effects of being called "Mommy and Daddy's chubby little angel." Everyone expected you to one day lose that baby fat. But that day never came, and now you are left with the disappointing realization that you'll never attain the sticklike figure of model Kate Moss or actress Calista Flockhart (Ally McBeal). Now you must endure comments such as, "You have such a pretty face . . . if you only lost a few pounds."

When I was in college, I went out with a man who informed me that he usually didn't date people as "big" as me, but he was making an exception because he liked my smile. Talk about a backhanded compliment! Even though I walked away from this potentially unhealthy relationship, the tape of his stinging comment continued to play in my mind for many years. One little comment like that can set us up for a lifelong struggle with self-control. Wanting to measure up (or measure *down*) to society's ideal body image, many people fall into compulsive dieting, eating disorders, and disillusionment with self. Other times we might try to rebel and say, "I shouldn't have to live up to anyone's expectations." So we eat more in rebellion. Self-control is hindered by our ill-conceived images and our desire to live down past perceptions of ourselves.

I have never read any verse in Scripture spelling out what constitutes a perfect body image. There are no biblical specifications of how much we should weigh, what color our hair should be, or the sizes of our noses, ears, or feet. God is concerned with the condition of our hearts, not our physical features. Although we may never fit society's image, we are made in *His* image. The Creator of the universe loves us completely and unreservedly. Therefore, our basis for self-control should be to please our Father, not other people or society.

Tapping into the Power

We know that we are powerless to change without the help of God's Holy Spirit. But how are we given access to this power in our everyday lives? God has graciously provided many different avenues.

We have the example of Jesus Christ. Everyone is faced with temptation in life. Even Jesus wasn't exempt.

Matthew 4:2-10 tells us how Jesus was tempted by the Devil with food, power, and possessions. How did Jesus conquer the temptations? He relied upon the love of God and the wisdom of the Holy Spirit. He knew and used Scripture as His defense and strength. We can go to Jesus because He has been there. He understands the temptations we face.

We have prayer, which gives us access to God's abundant and incomparable power. Only God's power can help us overcome our human desires. Prayer aligns our will with God's will, thus causing self-control to become more natural to us. Prayer allows us to shift from our selfish purposes toward God and His purposes for our lives. Prayer gives us strength and encouragement.

We have others to guide us. God has given us flesh-and-blood, here-and-now help in the form of mentors. Without more-experienced women to share my burdens and blunders, I would have never been able to pull through my tough struggles.

Several years ago, my marriage seemed to be sucked into a quagmire. Divorce seemed to be the only answer. When I confided to my mentor, Delores, that I was considering divorce, she gently but strongly confronted me with the Word of God. She reminded me that incompatibility and strife are not included in God's allowances for divorce. I had the choice of going against God's Word or turning to Him for help in changing my desire to control my husband and my marriage. Delores's commitment to pray for me and my marriage — as well as her willingness to share about the tough times in her own — gradually enabled me to "let go and let God." I will always be grateful for strong, godly women like Delores whom God provides to help clean up our messes (and help us avoid a few).

We have books and other resources to help us. One trip

to the bookstore can encourage you and give you help when dealing with any self-control issue. Allow others' experiences to facilitate your search for self-control by reading their books. Billy Graham's book *Angels* has helped me learn to control my travel anxiety. He explains that throughout the Bible are stories of how God used angels to protect His people from danger. God created angels to come to our aid and to protect us in times of fear and temptation. During our family travels, I always ask God to send His angels around the car, the airplane, or whatever mode of transportation we use. What a comfort it is to look out the window and see those angels in my mind's eye. I know angels are fervent protectors of God's children.

Another fabulous book, *She Can Laugh at the Days to Come* by Valerie Bell, helped alleviate some of the anxiety and jealousy preventing me from accepting the waning of my youth. This book encouraged me to believe that even though I no longer have a muscular, taut body and hair dye is a staple in my cupboard, I have a lot of living to do!

Self-control will always be a struggle because we are all human, and humans like things their own way. But just as David prevailed over Goliath, you, too, can triumph in your battle for self-control. Look to God and every tool He offers. Make it a daily effort to use those tools, knowing that He is with you, wanting you to receive blessings. Allow yourself to break free of your self-imposed bondage, and lavish yourself with the gift of living in freedom—the freedom you will receive when you place your life in the hands of Jesus Christ.

DIGGING DEEPER

1. What misconceptions did you have about self-control before reading this chapter?

2. Do you think women in the workforce face different self-control issues than women working at home? What might those issues be?

3. What do the following Scriptures tell you about God's view of image?
   Genesis 1:27

   Romans 8:29

   2 Timothy 1:7

   1 Peter 3:3-4

How does your perception of your image differ from these examples?

4. Had you considered criticism and judgment of others a self-control issue before reading this chapter? What do you believe causes us to criticize one another?

5. Explain what the following Scriptures teach you about criticism and judgment.
Proverbs 11:12; 15:28

Luke 6:37

Romans 2:1

6. God has given us resources to combat fear and addiction. According to the following Scriptures, what are they?
Mark 9:29; 11:24; Romans 15:30; Philippians 4:6

Psalm 34:7; Luke 4:10-11; Acts 12:11

Mark 2:3; Philippians 2:4; Titus 2:3-4

John 14:16; John 16:13; Romans 8:26

2 Samuel 22:33; Psalm 29:11; Isaiah 41:10

Colossians 2:13; 1 John 1:9

7. With what areas of self-control are you presently struggling? What plan can you set in motion to address these areas? In what ways might a mentor support you in these struggles?

8. Galatians 5:13-26 describes two lifestyles — one controlled by the sinful nature, the other controlled by the Spirit of God. List the behaviors of each way of life:

Sinful Nature   Spirit of God

_____   _____

_____   _____

_____   _____

_____   _____

_____   _____

9. Describe the nature of the following Bible characters: Cain and Abel (Genesis 4)

Sarai and Hagar (Genesis 16)

Miriam and Moses (Numbers 12)

Samson and Delilah (Judges 16)

Chapter Five

PURE AS THE DRIVEN SNOW

Purity Inside and Out

BY JANET COX

Then [the older women] can train the younger
women to . . . be . . . pure.

Titus 2:4-5

I enjoy looking into God's Word and peeling back the
layers to learn the best meaning of a passage. That is
what we will be doing with this short phrase: *be pure.*
As we do this, we will gain a better understanding of what
the Bible means by being pure, discover roadblocks to living a life of purity, and learn some ways to grow in our own
purity. We will start by examining two kinds of outward
purity, one in the near past and the other in Jesus' day.

Several years ago, I went with two friends to a conference at Asbury College and Seminary near Lexington,
Kentucky. Our motel was about twenty miles from the
college, so each day my friends and I drove through the

beautiful Kentucky countryside. We always noticed a place called the Shaker Village of Pleasant Hills. *Who were the Shakers?* we wondered. Our curiosity got the best of us one day, so we stopped at this National Historic Landmark to learn more.

We took the self-guided tour and discovered that Pleasant Hill is a restored Shaker village, and we discovered many interesting facts about the Shakers' simple, devout, creative, and orderly life.

Their lifestyle fascinated me. Later I found a book on the subject called *Simple Gifts: A Memoir of a Shaker Village* by June Sprigg. In it, Sprigg shares her experiences living in a Shaker colony for several summers. I loved reading about their uncomplicated lifestyle. This paragraph from her book gives a brief look at it:

> Shakers were famous in America for their unusual communal, celibate lifestyle, for the dance worship that simultaneously entertained and scandalized observers from the World, for the prosperity of their extensive farms and enterprises, and for the excellence of their products, which included vegetables seeds, brooms and brushes, botanic medicines, chairs, bonnets, buckets and oval wooden boxes. Over time, their steadfast commitment to peacefulness, charity, and honesty won them grudging admiration.[1]

Their motto was "hands to work and hearts for God." Their lifestyle could be described as one of purity. They espoused high ideals, celibacy, perfection in their work, separation from the world, and daily worship and meditation. The cleanliness and orderliness of their lifestyle and village were beyond reproach. It almost gave the indication that they were trying to create a heaven on earth.

However, their doctrine was clearly not a biblical or Christian one. One of the main tenets of their faith was that Christ's second coming would be as a woman. They also believed it was possible to establish a perfect society.

Celibacy proved to be a problem for the Shakers. They believed in sexual abstinence, not just sexual purity. Thus they did not marry nor did they have children to repopulate and continue the community. They took the idea of living a life of purity to such an extreme that it led to their own extinction! This certainly is not God's plan for living a pure life.

From all outward appearances, the Shakers looked pure; they were morally faultless, uncontaminated by the "world," simple, honest, and apparently lacking any form of self-interest. It reminds me of some religious groups in the Bible that held a similar idea of purity.

The Pharisees were an excellent New Testament example of living an outwardly pure life. Jesus gives a discourse on true purity versus the ceremonial cleanliness they had learned by tradition (see Mark 7:1-8). Their cleanliness was not for the sake of good hygiene but to rid themselves of any moral pollution. The Pharisees had been taught that moral defilement came by touching unclean things, so they religiously practiced washing with water for ceremonial purity.

Here is an account of Jesus confronting them:

And as He spoke, a certain Pharisee asked Him to dine with him. So He went in and sat down to eat. And when the Pharisee saw it, he marveled that He had not first washed before dinner.

Then the Lord said to him, "Now you Pharisees make the outside of the cup and dish clean, but your inward part is full of greed and wickedness. Foolish ones! Did not He who made the outside make the inside also? But rather give alms of such things as you have; then indeed all things are clean to you." (Luke 11:37-41, NKJV)

A clean environment or a clean body is not evidence of a pure life or mind. Purity comes from within and flows out of the heart. Purity of thought leads to purity of speech and behavior.

The Biblical Meaning of Purity

In searching the Scriptures for passages that speak of purity, I found fifteen Hebrew words in the Old Testament and three Greek words in the New Testament that are translated into English as *pure*. Some of the Hebrew terms relate to emptying out or being clean. *Baker's Evangelical Dictionary of Biblical Theology* gives the following definition: "Purity is the sense of being blameless, guiltless, or of innocent behavior. The verb appears about forty times and most occurrences relate to ethical, moral or forensic purity."

Our focus will be on the New Testament treatment of *pure*. The three Greek words translated as *pure* are *katharos, eilikrines,* and *hagnos* and are defined as follows, according to the *Spirit Filled Life Bible*:

Katharos, meaning ethical purity or cleanliness, is found for example in Matthew 5:8 — "Blessed are the pure in heart, for they will see God."

Eilikrines is defined as "free from falsehood and hidden motives"; it is found in 2 Peter 3:1 — "Dear friends, this is now my second letter to you. I have written both of them as reminders to stimulate you to wholesome [pure] thinking."

Hagnos, which means morally faultless or undefiled, is the word used in 1 John 3:3 — "Everyone who has this hope in him purifies himself, just as he is pure." The word in Titus 2:5 is *hagnos,* the same as the one used in 1 John 3:3. It is from the same root as *hagios,* meaning *holy.* "The adjective describes a person or thing as clean, modest, pure, undefiled, morally faultless, and without blemish. Christ's ability to overcome temptation and remain pure makes him a role model for all believers."[2]

For this chapter, we will define the word *pure* as "modest, morally faultless, and holy."

Impurity in Our Culture

Now that we have a grasp on the definition, let us explore what this means in our everyday life. Perhaps the easiest way to do this is to look at the opposite of purity: impurity. Society today tends to gloss over impure living by using a contemporary phrase to describe a situation, making the unacceptable seem acceptable.

At one time, an unmarried man and woman living together were said to be "shacking up," a rather uncomplimentary term. But now it is called "cohabitation." This supposedly makes it acceptable. A little padding of the expense account (stealing) is acceptable because the company "owes it to you." Getting too much change back on a purchase is "their" fault, so there is no need to return it. Words such as *adultery* and *fornication* are almost foreign in our current vocabulary. We have taken these harsh words and watered them down to make the impure seem acceptable.

Two New Testament verses tell us in a straightforward way how to deal with impurity. Ephesians 5:3 says, "But among you *there must not be even a hint* of sexual immorality, or *of any kind of impurity,* or of greed, because these are improper for God's holy people" (emphasis added). And Colossians 3:5 says, "*Put to death,* therefore, whatever belongs to your earthly nature: sexual immorality, *impurity,* lust, evil desires and greed, which is idolatry" (emphasis added). Though these verses are not heeded by many of us today, they are still true.

Refining the Impure

What can we do to eliminate impurity from our lives? We can draw close to God and let Him refine us. God is willing and anxious to help us grow in purity, but this will most likely require testing. Job, the Old Testament warrior of suffering, says, "But he knows the way that I take; when he has tested me, I will come forth as gold" (Job 23:10). Purifying often comes through the fiery furnace of trials and testing in our everyday lives.

I am reminded of the story of an old goldsmith who lived in Asia over a hundred years ago. He used an ancient method for refining gold. First he prepared a special mixture of salt, tamarind fruit, and burnt brick dust in a crude crucible that he then heated over a red-hot charcoal fire. Next he dropped the lump of ore into the mixture and let it boil until the gold was separated from the ore. When it had cooled, he was able to remove the piece of gold. The gold was now separate but not pure. He then put it in his crucible and made the fire hotter and hotter in order to remove the impurities. When asked how he knew when the gold was pure, he replied that it was purified when he could see his face reflected in it.

This is an excellent illustration of how the impurity in our lives needs to be continually refined through testing, so that we will shine as a reflection of God and His love.

Beginning the Journey

We start this process when we come to Christ with all of our impurity. As we confess our sins and pray to receive

Him into our heart, there is newness, a peace, a freedom from the sin in our life. Now comes the hard part: actively pursuing purity. It never comes easily; it takes concentrated effort.

One reason this is so difficult is explained in 1 Peter 5:8: "Your enemy the devil prowls around like a roaring lion looking for someone to devour." Satan is always ready to trip us. One of his favorite weapons is aimed at our minds. If he can get us to doubt what we know to be true, his job is much easier. This mode of operation goes all the way back to Eve and her encounter with him as he was disguised as a serpent in the Garden of Eden. Genesis 3:1-13 relates this story for us:

> Now the serpent was more crafty than any of the wild animals the LORD God had made. He said to the woman, "Did God really say, 'You must not eat from any tree in the garden'?"
>
> The woman said to the serpent, "We may eat fruit from the trees in the garden, but God did say, 'You must not eat fruit from the tree that is in the middle of the garden, and you must not touch it, or you will die.'"
>
> "You will not surely die," the serpent said to the woman. "For God knows that when you eat of it your eyes will be opened, and you will be like God, knowing good and evil."
>
> When the woman saw that the fruit of the tree was good for food and pleasing to the eye, and also desirable for gaining wisdom, she took some and ate it. She also gave some to her husband, who was with her, and he ate it. Then the eyes of both of them were opened, and they realized they were naked; so they sewed fig leaves together and made coverings for themselves.

> Then the man and his wife heard the sound of
> the LORD God as he was walking in the garden in
> the cool of the day, and they hid from the LORD
> God among the trees of the garden. But the
> LORD God called to the man, "Where are you?"
> He answered, "I heard you in the garden, and
> I was afraid because I was naked; so I hid."
> And he said, "Who told you that you were
> naked? Have you eaten from the tree that I com-
> manded you not to eat from?"
> The man said, "The woman you put here
> with me—she gave me some fruit from the tree,
> and I ate it."
> Then the LORD God said to the woman,
> "What is this you have done?"
> The woman said, "The serpent deceived me,
> and I ate."

Eve had it right when she said, "The serpent deceived me." This often happens to us, too. It's like a slippery slope: We get too close to the edge and then down we go.

Temptation is composed of two elements: our inward desire and the outward circumstances around us. James 1:13-14 explains the dilemma this way: "When tempted, no one should say, 'God is tempting me.' For God cannot be tempted by evil, nor does he tempt anyone; but each one is tempted when, by his own evil desire, he is dragged away and enticed." When we allow our wrong desires to go unchecked and find ourselves in the wrong circumstance, we have given in to temptation.

The good news is that we are not without God's power in our life to resist sin. Call a mentor to pray with you. Get out your Bible and memorize appropriate passages. Join a group of women who will provide support and accountability.

Roadblocks Along the Way

So many things thwart our efforts to be pure. You need to become aware of the pitfalls so you are better able to chart your way. Satan's first line of attack is to put a thought in your mind, maybe just a fleeting thought, but one that can be a seed that starts to grow. Almost before you know what is happening, you are acting out what only moments before was just a passing thought. Our old nature—the Bible calls it our flesh or our carnal nature—is still with us, and many times we yield to its influence.

STRUGGLES WITH OUR THOUGHT LIFE

There are many hazards today that can entice us away from the pathway of purity. Modern technologies such as TVs, CDs, DVDs, VCRs, and the Internet can bring impure images and messages into our minds. Twenty-first-century communication methods and entertainment arenas are awesome and easily accessible—movies, concerts, magazines, books, newspapers—and none of them are intrinsically evil. However, you need to develop discernment to keep your heart and mind pure when it comes to choosing your entertainment.

One incident concerning my television viewing habits was a defining point in my life. I attended a special church service in which we were challenged to edit our television watching. I was not at that time, nor am I now, much of a TV person (maybe because my husband always has the remote control). But at the time, I was watching a certain soap opera that came on each afternoon while my three-year-old daughter was napping. I would lie down on the sofa and invite my four-year-old son, who was almost too big for a nap, to sit in the room and play so I could watch him while I rested. Of course this particular soap had the usual dose of illicit sex, adultery, and lying.

When I heard the speaker's challenge, I became convicted that this wasn't the lifestyle I wanted modeled before my eyes or my children's. I knew I needed to change my viewing habits. By God's grace, I was able to stop watching that soap opera that very day. That's saying quite a bit because, as you may know, those shows can be addictive!

This incident caused my husband and me to become more discerning about our television viewing in the evenings. We decided we would not watch any shows made for mature audiences until the children were in bed. The shows we did watch were mild compared to the shows that are splattered across the television screen today.

I challenge you to examine your television viewing habits. What type of messages and pictures are you bringing into your life and the life of your family? Our eyes have been called the window to our soul, and our minds are definitely affected by what we see. As Psalm 101:3 says, "I will set before my eyes no vile thing."

SPEAKING THE THOUGHTS—OUR SPEECH

Many times we can have a thought in our minds and not acknowledge it or dwell on it, but then all of a sudden it slips out of our mouth! This often happens when we are chatting with our friends. It is called gossip. We may have no intention of passing along something we heard; then a person's name comes up in the conversation and we blurt out what we heard. The gossip seed starts to grow!

One of many verses reminding us to guard our tongue is 1 Peter 3:10: "Whoever would love life and see good days must keep his tongue from evil and his lips from deceitful speech." We must also refrain from dirty or evil language in speaking or writing. There is no redeeming value in repeating someone's vulgar joke. In fact, close your mind to it as soon you hear it. In today's computer age, our written words can be quickly and easily sent to unknown persons by way of Internet chat rooms. It seems so easy to slip in a sexual comment as you type, reasoning that you will never meet this anonymous person face to face, so why not have a little fun. This promotes impure thinking in you as well as another.

BATTLING OUR BEHAVIOR PATTERNS

Pick up a copy of almost any Christian magazine and you will find a story of someone dealing with an addiction or unhealthy habit. Activities that even Christians have become trapped in include horoscopes, new age activities, witchcraft, drugs, alcohol, gambling, and sexual sins. Susan Hunt writes in *Spiritual Mothering:*

> Addictions of any kind are a contradiction to self-control, purity and discipline. With the prolifera-tion of addictions today, we need women who are exercising discipline and who are imposing upon themselves standards of purity in all areas of their lives. Among women, the problems of substance abuse, promiscuity, eating disorders, and soap opera addictions demand a response. The reason-able response for Christian women is to coura-geously bring their lives under the authority of God's Word and to live according to His stan-dards of purity.[3]

Overindulgence in our lives is in direct opposition to living a life of purity. Many women struggle with some kind of addiction and many others have been touched by the addictions of a family member or friend. Overcoming an addiction requires help from others. This is definitely a job for a mentor!

Perhaps the most common addiction among Christian

women is evidenced in their love affair with food. We point our finger at many others around us for their lack of self-control and harmful habits but don't see our own problem.

Even as I write this, I realize the struggle that goes on within my own heart over how to live a life of purity and how to influence others in a positive way rather than pulling them down. Many times we want our own way just because we want it. Yet I know that God's way is best, and to struggle with Him only prolongs the battle. In the end, He will change my will to His (see Philippians 2:13). There is a constant need to choose purity—in thought, speech, and behavior.

Growing in Purity

Jesus said, "Blessed are the pure in heart, for they will see God" (Matthew 5:8). Our main reason for growing in purity is to grow closer to God. What's more, as we grow closer to God, we will grow in purity. Psalm 24:3-4 explains this for us: "Who may ascend the hill of the LORD? Who may stand in his holy place? He who has clean hands and a pure heart."

Here are four ways that will help you GROW toward a pure life:

1. **G**o to God's Word: read, study, and memorize it.
2. **R**emember to pray and confess.
3. **O**bey the voice and prompting of the Holy Spirit.
4. **W**alk with a mentor.

GO TO GOD'S WORD
Our number-one weapon in our struggle to live a life of purity is God's Word. A verse that can encourage you lest

you become discouraged by your lack of perfection is Psalm 119:9. The writer asks the question, "How can a young man [woman] keep his [her] way pure?" Verses 9 and 11 answer: "By living according to your word. . . . I have hidden your word in my heart that I might not sin against you." This gives us one reason for the necessity of developing purity in our lives: so that we will not sin against God.

The key is to commit the Word to memory so it is in your *heart*. Purity is an inward evidence of God in your life. God has shown us, in His Word, the path to purity. He has set the standards for a pure life as well as creating us with a longing to experience Him in a more intimate way.

As author and ministry leader Jerry Bridges says, "It is very clear in Scripture that if we are to experience and see God, then we must be pure and holy. To be holy is to be morally blameless, to be separated from sin and therefore consecrated to God."[4]

REMEMBER TO PRAY AND CONFESS

Prayer and purity are closely related. Most likely we come to God in prayer, confessing and asking forgiveness for our failure to live purely. Perhaps we have not spoken the truth or maybe we cheated our boss by leaving too early from our job. Then, when we realize the wrong we are capable of, we ask God to give us strength to do the right thing.

We find it easy to pray for things we want or things that concern us, but confessing our sin requires more concerted effort. Pray for God's help and direction in your life, and listen. Pray expectantly (see 1 John 5:14-15)!

Hear that inaudible voice reminding you, "You left work fifteen minutes early yesterday and cheated your boss by not giving him what he paid you for." Confess it and ask God to help you do better from now on. You may find that the next day you are busy right up until time to leave work. This answered prayer motivates more prayer. With the joy of each answered prayer, our muscles of faith grow stronger.

There are many prayers in the Scriptures and many books of prayers, but finding a mentor who will pray with you is valuable. God is waiting for us to call on Him: "Call to me and I will answer you" (Jeremiah 33:3).

OBEY GOD'S DIRECTION

Living in obedience to God's Word is not something we learn quickly or easily. We need to start with small steps and proceed to bigger ones as our faith grows. Obedience is an exercise of faith. Perhaps we could start with such a passage as Psalm 34:12-13: "Whoever of you loves life and desires to see many good days, keep your tongue from evil and your lips from speaking lies." This is one we all can heed, and it includes a promise if we obey the command. (If this seems too tame for you, the Ten Commandments are an excellent standard for our walk of purity.)

Now ask God to make you more sensitive to the things you say to others. You might be surprised what happens. Christ has provided help for us to obey God by giving us His Holy Spirit. The Spirit speaks the voice of God to our hearts. Sometimes that voice is still and small, and other times He calls our name loudly. If we are sincere, we will know, without a doubt, what we should change and confess; and then we must obey wholeheartedly.

In his classic devotional book, *My Utmost for His Highest*, Oswald Chambers writes:

> Obey God in the things He shows you, and instantly the next thing is opened up. One reads tomes on the work of the Holy Spirit, when five

minutes of drastic obedience would make things as clear as a sunbeam. "I suppose I shall understand these things some day!" You can understand them now. It is not study that does it, but obedience. The tiniest fragment of obedience, and heaven opens and the profoundest truths of God are yours straight away. God will never reveal more truth about Himself until you obey what you already know.[5]

Walk with a Mentor

The admonition to "be pure" seems vague and elusive when we first read it. However, as we delve into what is written about purity elsewhere in the Bible, we begin to see more clearly the impurity in our lives. God knows how we stray from ethical, moral, and spiritual purity and so has given us His directions.

Remember this if the struggle is hard: "Truly the choice is ours. What will we choose? Will we accept our responsibility and discipline ourselves to live in habitual obedience to the will of God? Will we persevere in the face of frequent failure, resolving never to give up?"[6]

People have long attempted to clean up the outside of their lives to give the appearance of being completely clean. The Shakers and Pharisees had this in common with many others. They wanted the world to think of them as the picture of purity. But no matter how good a front we put on for others, God knows our hearts.

We need to continue to seek Him each day and He will give us the victory. The joy of knowing Him is worth all our efforts. Personal purity is indeed worth the struggle.

DIGGING DEEPER

1. Before reading this chapter, how would you have defined purity?

2. What kind of person do you picture when you think of one who lives a life of purity?

3. How difficult do you think it is to live a life of purity in today's society?

4. Read Philippians 4:8-9. What type of thoughts should we fill our minds with?

5. List the three Greek words translated *pure* in the New Testament (explained on pages 106-107) and give a present-day example of each.

a.

b.

c.

6. Is being tempted a sin? Read James 1:13-15 and explain in your own words how we are prone to sin.

7. Our *thoughts,* our *speech,* and our *behavior* are areas that need to be purified. Which area is referred to in each of the following verses? Proverbs 15:26

Proverbs 20:11

Matthew 12:34

Mark 7:20-23

James 1:27

8. How does 1 Peter 1:22 indicate that you can purify your soul?

9. Read 2 Timothy 2:22. How can you flee lust?

10. What is the area of temptation referred to in 1 Timothy 6:9-11?

Describe how the destructive process from thought to action can make a difference in the way we handle our money.

11. Based upon this chapter, what steps can you take to mature in purity?

12. List the purpose and benefits of living a life of purity.

13. Choose one area in your personal life in which you want to grow in purity (for example, thought life). What actions will you take to improve (for example, "I will stop watching my favorite soap opera for at least thirty days")?

Chapter Six

MORE THAN CHORES

The Ministry of Housekeeping

BY TAMMY EAGAN

Then [the older women] can train the younger women . . . to be busy at home.

Titus 2:4-5

Currently, my family and I live in a large, four-bedroom home about a hundred miles north of London in the English countryside. The view out my office window is lovely. As I glance to the east, I see several other brick-and-stone homes, some new and some very old. The village church steeple rises above the red tiled rooftops and seems to glow as it reflects the morning sun. A quaint stone fence lines the back of our property. Beyond is a breathtaking view of rolling farm fields that, with England's climate, remain varying shades of green all year 'round. After a year of living here, the scene still overwhelms me.

There's another view that, for different reasons, also overwhelms me: the chaos and mess on the *inside* of the house! With five active people living here, the effect is often similar to a scene you might find in my homeland—the aftermath of a good ol' Illinois tornado. It's not always all that bad, but it seems an uphill battle to keep things in some kind of order.

This month has been particularly difficult. In addition to wrapping up my portion of this book, I started a new job as associate minister of small groups at a large church. This new challenge is the culmination of years of training and the answer to my prayers. My children—ages seventeen, fifteen, and eleven—are happy for me. My husband cheers me on and is supportive in practical ways. However, no matter how exciting my ministry is for us, the fact remains that someone has to take care of our home.

Right now, as I type, there's a strange man in my house. He's here for our annual gas safety check, which is required by law. After this busy week, it was necessary for me to scramble around and clean up a bit before he arrived. I thought I was doing well, picking up the area near the boiler, wiping down the stovetop, and clearing a path through the living room to the gas fireplace. Boy, was I in for a surprise when he informed me that to complete his inspection, it was necessary to go through *every* room in the house and drain the radiators. *Ugh!* As he worked in the downstairs, I slipped up to my bedroom and quickly made the bed and picked up some of the clothes I had strewn around during the week. I know the gas safety inspector could care less about my housekeeping, but I felt more comfortable with some rooms at least up to the level of decency. As for my teenagers' rooms . . . the inspector will just have to understand, and hopefully he won't trip over anything.

For today's women, the directive to "be busy at home"

might seem odd. It is rarely a problem for any of us to find enough to do. The work never ends! Initially, the topic of housekeeping might also appear a bit boring and mundane. After all, it doesn't seem very "spiritual." In reality, though, it is a very important subject to explore. I hope to approach it with some biblical principles, practical advice, and a healthy dose of humor. Consider the contrasting views of housework from biblical times and our modern era:

> She makes coverings for her bed; she is clothed in fine linen and purple. (Proverbs 31:22)

> You make the beds, you do the dishes, and six months later you have to start all over again. (Joan Rivers)

> When it snows, she has no fear for her household; for all of them are clothed in scarlet. (Proverbs 31:21)

> Housework can't kill you, but why take the risk? I buried a lot of my ironing in the back yard. (Phyllis Diller)

> She sees that her trading is profitable, and her lamp does not go out at night. (Proverbs 31:18)

> Cleanliness is not next to godliness. It isn't even in the same neighborhood. No one has ever gotten a religious experience out of removing burned-on cheese from the grill of the toaster oven. (Erma Bombeck)

> She watches over the affairs of her household and does not eat the bread of idleness. (Proverbs 31:27)

Housework is like cleaning fish. No matter how often you do it, it still stinks. (Vicki Lawrence as Thelma Harper in *Mama's Family*)

Give her the reward she has earned, and let her works bring her praise at the city gate. (Proverbs 31:31)

Housekeeping ain't no joke. (Louisa May Alcott)

Housework! We make light of it, have fun with it, delegate it, avoid it, and obsess about it. In many homes, for better or for worse, it's the woman who usually carries the load. Perhaps this is only natural, as comedian Dave Barry states: "Women, for hormonal reasons, can see individual dirt molecules, whereas men tend not to notice them until they join together in clumps large enough to support commercial agriculture."[1]

Hopefully, things are changing in dual-career households, where both partners are working outside the home. It would be ideal if the work were divided fifty-fifty or something close to that, but in real-life partnerships of any kind the goal of perfect equality gets a bit unwieldy and creates frustration. This chapter will deal with the *reality* that today, as in the apostle Paul's day, women are generally the domestic managers of the home.

Why does housework get so overwhelming when we consider all the time-saving appliances available to us? My parents laugh as they tell about a workday in their home. Dad was in the yard and went inside to recruit some help from my mother. When he asked her to give him a hand, she calmly informed him that she was quite involved with her own chores.

"I'm cleaning the oven, doing the laundry, and washing the dishes," she replied.

What baffled my father was that while she said this, she was sitting on the sofa thumbing through a magazine. Her response was true enough—the dishwasher was running, the dryer was humming, and the oven was locked into the self-clean mode. If my mother had been performing all those tasks simultaneously fifty years ago, the scene would have been quite different. I suspect that after a good laugh Mom went outside to help Dad in the yard.

We can be thankful that we don't have as much physical labor as our grandmothers. However, we still find keeping up with our homes and families quite stressful. In her book *More Work for Mother,* Ruth Schwartz Cowen says that many of today's conveniences have created more work in the home, not less.[2] After an in-depth study of housework since the 1600s, Cowen reached an unexpected conclusion: housework has become more difficult than ever before.

When considering three major areas of housework—cooking, cleaning, and laundry—Cowen concluded that these chores have become more difficult for two reasons. First, expectations and standards have risen to a level unimaginable in previous generations. We expect our homes to be cleaner, our wardrobes to be more varied, and our meals more complicated than our ancestors'. Second, our lifestyle has added many demands on families that were nonexistent in years past. Our great-grandmothers did not contend with carpools, organized children's activities, or demands from their careers. The bottom line, according to Cowen, is more work for women, not less.

As we look forward to even more time-saving devices on the horizon, there is some concern about whether they will simplify our lives or make them more complex. Science writer Susan McCarthy says, "Technology will supply amazing new devices and nifty processes to make housework faster and easier. The dark side is the likelihood that the easier housework becomes, the more we'll invent new housework tasks. No sooner were washing machines invented than people took it into their heads to change their clothes more often."[3]

A Biblical View of Homemaking

When speaking of the care of the home, the Bible directs its instruction to women. This is found in our study of Titus 2: "Train the younger women . . . to be busy at home." One version simply states, to "be homemakers." Another exhortation of this kind is found in 1 Timothy 5:14, where Paul says he desires the young widows to marry, bear children, and manage the home. This, he says, will keep them from becoming idle and getting into trouble. Keep in mind that in Paul's day the options for women were extremely limited. His directive to these women was not to keep them barefoot, pregnant, and cleaning up after the rest of the family, but to keep them from falling into sin because of idleness. Paul's concern was for the women and the health of the local church, because both were coming under the threat of false teaching that was fueled by idle women. Take heart, sisters, Paul was not blaming the entire problem on women. In his report to Timothy, Paul identifies the false teachers themselves as men (see 1 Timothy 1:3).

Commenting on Titus 2:4-5, renowned theologian John R. W. Stott says,

> It would not be legitimate to base on this word
> either a stay-at-home stereotype for all women, or
> a prohibition of wives being also professional
> women. What is rather affirmed is that if a
> woman accepts the vocation of marriage, and has
> a husband and children, she will love and not

neglect them. J. B. Phillips' word "home lovers" sums up well what Paul has in mind. What he [Paul] is opposing is not a wife's pursuit of a profession, but the "habit of being idle and going about from house to house."[4]

Sadly, some have attempted to place limitations on women based on what the Bible says about them caring for the home. As we consider what the Bible says about women and homemaking, let's consider what Paul did *not* say.

Paul did not teach that women couldn't be active outside the home, either in volunteer work or a professional career. This kind of restriction would be a contradiction of the excellent wife described in Proverbs 31. This lady was involved in real estate investments (verse 16) and her own manufacturing business (verse 24), while still maintaining a respectable home. In Luke 8:1-3, we read that there were women traveling with Jesus and the Twelve and "helping to support them out of their own means." We aren't given specific details of how these women earned their income, and it may have been household money provided by husbands. It's more important to see that these women were significantly involved in activities outside their home—Jesus' ministry in this case—and were able to support His ministry financially by some means. Jesus did not prohibit this. In Acts 16:13-15, we meet Lydia, a prominent businesswoman known to be a worshiper of God. After her baptism and the conversion of her entire household, she offered hospitality to Paul, Silas, and Timothy.

Paul did not say that men couldn't help with the housework or that housework is strictly women's work. In fact, we find in the New Testament the admonition for husbands to be considerate to their wives and treat them with respect (see 1 Peter 3:7). God designed marriage to be a partnership in which each one honors the other. A Christian man is to love his wife as Christ loves the church (see Ephesians 5:25). Obviously, this attitude encompasses a broad range of life issues and practices, of which housework is only a small part. We can conclude, though, that a man who puts himself above doing what he perceives to be "woman's work" in the home is not exhibiting a loving, giving attitude toward his wife. This kind of pride is such a contrast to the powerful actions of Jesus as He took up a servant's towel and washed His disciples' feet. For men today, demonstrating an attitude of unselfishness and humility might mean running the vacuum!

I am encouraged when I see examples of couples working together to take care of their home. My sister, Tina, is married, has two children, and works full time as a manager for a large insurance company. She and her husband, Tim, who also works long hours, share many of the household chores. It's common on Saturday mornings for Tim to be out with their two little girls doing the weekly grocery shopping while Tina is at home cleaning. Tim is the King of Coupons at their house, and you can always count on him to know which supermarket offers the best prices. He does most of the weeknight cooking as he is usually first to arrive home after picking up the girls from school. The girls are growing up seeing their parents working together as a team (although my sister is afraid she needs to do more in the kitchen; one of her daughters announced that her mommy is a good cook because "She makes the *best* microwave popcorn!").

Paul was not devaluing women or giving them second-class status in the home. In God's sight, a woman's spiritual position in Christ is no different from a man's. Paul stated, "There is neither Jew nor Greek, slave nor free, male nor female, for you are all one in Christ Jesus" (Galatians 3:28).

In Paul's day, the functional roles of men and women may have been different. In our day the distinctions are fading, but no matter what our functional role, our value to God is the same. *We* are the ones who struggle with the distinction between *what we do* and *who we are.*

In twenty-first-century America, women are free to explore callings away from the home as never before, but the reality remains that someone must care for the home. It seems that most often it is the woman who has the passion, creativity, and vision to make her home a fantastic place. As women, let's make the most of the gifts God's given us!

What Does the Bible Say About Work?

As we take a look at how we are to be busy at home, let us first examine our attitudes. Ephesians 6:7-8 offers a general principle that applies to all activities: "Serve wholeheartedly, as if you were serving the Lord, not men, because you know that the Lord will reward everyone for whatever good he does." Do you work in your home joyfully or with frustration? When our attitude gets negative, it is often because we have forgotten for whom we are working. If our focus is on all that we do for others and what they don't do for us in return, it is only a matter of time before contentment is replaced with resentment. On the other hand, if we focus on doing all things as if we were serving God, we are able to persevere and keep a joyful spirit. Let's look at a few other biblical principles concerning work:

God values work. One of the results of the Fall of man is stated in Genesis 3:19: "By the sweat of your brow you will eat your food." It is true that when sin entered the world, work became more difficult, but work itself was not a part of the curse. Before Adam and Eve sinned, God gave them work. He delegated to them the responsibility of taking care of creation. Therefore, work and responsibility were part of God's original plan for humankind.

In Ecclesiastes 3:22, King Solomon wrote, "So I saw that there is nothing better for a man than to enjoy his work." Rather than being a curse, our work is a gift—something we can enjoy.

God does not see some jobs as more important than others. Perhaps it's human nature for us to view some kinds of work as being more meaningful than others. Certain jobs in our culture carry a greater level of status and respect. We need to remember that these are the attitudes of people and are not God's values. Often homemakers feel that their work is not very important or prestigious. If we can adopt God's view of the value of homemaking, the opinions of others will have less impact.

All work has a certain amount of futility. Ecclesiastes 2:17-23 speaks specifically about the futility of work. The author seems particularly concerned that, after all his hard work, he will have to leave his accomplishments to someone else who could be a fool and destroy it all. Work was cursed after the Fall, and we read in Genesis 3:18 that the ground would thereafter produce "thorns and thistles." More futility is described in verse 19: "By the sweat of your brow you will eat your food until you return to the ground, since from it you were taken; for dust you are and to dust you will return." No wonder we often feel the exasperation of King Solomon, who said, "All of it is meaningless, a chasing after the wind" (Ecclesiastes 2:17).

I remember a time when I worked in a busy physician's office. I noticed how many routine and mundane tasks this doctor performed each day. Although he found his work rewarding, there was a certain amount of drudgery involved. It was interesting to me that, alongside the joys of this profession, there were also the hassles and frustrations found in any other job. This perspective helped me as I went home to deal with my awaiting chores.

When we consider our housework, we sometimes get a case of self-pity. It's laborious, often boring, and much of it feels futile because it has to be repeated continuously. To make matters worse, there is often a lack of appreciation from family members. It has helped me to keep in mind that all professions carry some, if not all, of these same frustrations. There are so many joys related to taking care of a home; let's focus on those.

Homemaking: The Fairy Tale Meets Reality

I began my career as a full-time homemaker eighteen years ago during my pregnancy with our first child. It was a time I greatly anticipated. As a young girl, I had many ideas of what I wanted to "be" when I grew up. My dream profession changed from year to year. But what I wanted most of all was to be a good wife, mother, and homemaker.

I wanted my children to grow up with warm memories of a comfortable home. I envisioned my husband coming home each evening to an inviting sanctuary. Our home would be neat and well decorated, and there would always be home-baked cookies waiting for the kids after school. The aroma of the evening meal would fill the house as it slowly roasted in the oven. We wouldn't spend our weekends or evenings doing "chores," because I would finish them all during the day while my husband did his bit at the office.

This seemed like a reasonable goal to me. I had always been a hard worker. During my high school and college years, I worked long hours at various jobs while finishing my education. After graduation, I maintained a demanding pace as a radiographer at a busy trauma center. After a few years of inhaling darkroom chemicals (not intentionally), lifting patients and equipment, and running from one call to another, it seemed to me that working in my own home would be an extended holiday.

Then came reality! I had no idea how difficult it is to run a home. Children required much more time and emotional energy than I had anticipated. I didn't know that my family would not "arise and call [me] blessed" every day. I hadn't anticipated how lonely and isolated I would feel. I was beginning to think that perhaps my delusions about home life were the result of breathing in all those darkroom chemicals in the X-ray lab.

Today I can laugh at a foot-in-mouth comment my husband, Tom, once made. Our daughter, Valerie, was a few weeks old. Along with some "new baby" photos, we developed another unidentified roll of film that we had discovered in the back of a drawer. We were pleasantly surprised that the prints turned out to be some great pictures taken on our honeymoon four years prior. As Tom flipped through the stack of photos, I sat on the sofa nursing our newborn, gently cradling her in my right arm. At the same time our two-year-old son, Kevin, was yanking on my left arm. He was crying after being disciplined for jumping on the furniture. Looking at the smiling new bride in the pictures and then looking back at me, Tom commented, "You were so relaxed and happy back then." As I looked down at the children attached to various parts of my body, I was faced with two choices: to laugh or to kill him. Needless to say, he's still living, but I think he might still have a bruised shin.

I, too, saw myself differently after becoming a wife and mother. I had always thought of myself as disciplined, motivated, and hard working. Others had described me as cheerful and laid-back. Now at home a different woman was emerging, one who would vacillate between procrastinating and working like a maniac to get caught up. In either situation, I was irritable and depressed. Perhaps this woman had been around all along, but when I was busy with my job outside the home, it was easier to ignore her.

I discovered that without the accountability that came from a supervisor and coworkers, I had no discipline. I didn't know how to schedule my work. In my former job, someone else had always scheduled it for me.

I also didn't know how to set boundaries with family and friends. I rarely asked for help, nor did I feel that I deserved it. I was inconsistent about taking care of myself spiritually, emotionally, and physically. If I were asked to serve in any way in my church or community, I rarely said no. I believed that because I did not "work," I surely must have time. I measured my success by unrealistic standards of what I *should* be doing or how things *ought* to be. I had wrongly attached my self-image to my performance in these areas. Though our family might have looked fine from a distance, up close my life was out of control.

My situation may have been a bit extreme. However, it has been my observation that many women struggle similarly with the demands of keeping a home. It seems to be human nature to have a problem finding balance in life. Like a pendulum, we swing from one extreme to another. Homemakers can fall into the extreme of the "messy" camp, living with a level of disorder that is not good. Some might go to the other extreme, becoming obsessively neat and striving to control their environment to the point that they cannot relax and their relationships suffer. It is important that we find a balance that is healthy for ourselves and our family.

How Do We Manage Our Homes?

Many good books have been written about the how-tos of housework. There are also workshops available at church retreats and other conferences for homemakers. Although

I still struggle sometimes, I have found some things that have helped me recover from my home hassles. I have chosen the acronym HOME to outline four of the basics: ask for help, obliterate comparisons, manage well, and escape occasionally.

HELP!

Ask for help. There are many reasons we don't do this often enough. We want things done right the *first* time. We want them done according to our schedule. Recruiting help requires forethought and planning. We may feel that we shouldn't need help because our home is our responsibility, or we may feel that we shouldn't have to ask because our families should know what needs to be done and do it. If you find yourself overwhelmed by doing nearly everything at your house, you need to ask for help. There are several sources you can draw from to get assistance.

The first, and sometimes the most difficult recruits, are those lovely people with whom we share our joys, our sorrows, our toothpaste, and our daily lives. Family members are often willing to help if asked calmly, in advance, and not just when we are impatient or in panic mode. When children are old enough, they can and should be working in the home — not just for Mom's benefit, but also for their own. Family psychologist John Rosemond says, "A family is an organization. As such, everyone in the family should have the equivalent of a job description."[5] Sharing household chores teaches responsibility and gives children a sense of belonging to the family. Eventually, they may gain appreciation for the amount of work required to keep their lives running smoothly.

Training children to participate in household chores will be more time consuming initially, while they are learning. In the long run, their help pays off. Start as soon as they are able. A two-year-old can be guided through the process of picking up her toys. A five-year-old can help you set the table if you provide some non-breakable dinner-ware for family meals. An eight-year-old can easily take out the trash, and by age twelve most children can be taught to accomplish almost any adult task.

A reward system can be helpful. Young children might relate to something simple like earning stars on a chart for helping Mommy each day. Their work is rewarded by a trip to the playground or some other special place. Older children are best motivated by cold, hard cash. However, sometimes children need to be reminded that they should help out not because they will receive a reward, but because it is their responsibility as a member of the family. Just as they receive the benefits of a comfortable home, they also need to contribute to its upkeep. You want to avoid a situation in which your teenager is asked to mow the lawn and he replies, "How much are you going to pay me?"

Often husbands are willing to share in the housework. When I was not working outside the home, I did not ask much of Tom. After putting in a long week at his job, he also volunteered in the music ministry at our church. He takes care of our family finances and most of the lawn and car care. He's also a great dad. When the kids were little he was the first to play games or watch cartoons with them. Frequently, Tom was willing to supervise their bath time or change a diaper so that I could rest or cook a meal.

Occasionally, we would swap jobs around the house. I remember one extremely hot summer when he was dreading mowing the grass, and I was exasperated with the never-ending loads of laundry. For a few weeks, we traded. He sat inside in the air conditioning with the kids while he folded towels and tiny pairs of underwear. I enjoyed time alone listening to tunes on my Walkman and mowing the grass. This was a win-win arrangement.

Several years ago, I began attending Bible college and working part time for the small-groups ministry at the church we attended at that time. Initially, this required some adjustment because for the majority of our married life I was primarily a full-time homemaker. When I started this new adventure, our kids were in school all day. I was pleased that my job and course schedule allowed me to be with them before and after school. However, my outside activities did require a bit more from me on the weekends and a few evenings each week. Obviously, I couldn't keep up with all the household chores I had been doing prior to this.

Tom was quite supportive of my new responsibilities. In fact, during trying times, when I was tempted to give up, he was my greatest encourager to hang in there and accept God's calling. As we discussed our schedules and the jobs that needed doing, we noticed that there were things that he enjoys doing more than I. For example, Tom enjoys shopping, or at least he doesn't mind it so much. He does most of the clothes shopping with our boys. He is usually the most willing to tackle the dreaded school supply list that comes around each autumn. He enjoys shopping for gifts, especially at Christmas. He even wraps the presents and does a much better job than I. He's willing to do the grocery shopping and would often take the kids along to give me some time alone.

I, too, support Tom by encouraging him in his work as an electrical engineer. I do my best to have a nice meal ready when he comes home in the evening. I adjust my schedule to allow him time to relax and to be involved in the music ministry he enjoys. We both make it a high priority to be at the kids' activities, and we're usually both at parent-teacher conferences, important concerts, or sporting events. We're not perfect at all this, but we try to maintain a good balance. Here are a few keys to recruiting your husband's help:

◆ Consider both of your schedules.
◆ Ask nicely.
◆ Find things that he enjoys, or at least doesn't mind so much.
◆ Make adjustments as needed.
◆ Look for win-win solutions.

The second option for getting help is to hire someone. The biggest hindrance to this is usually financial. Obviously, not everyone can afford such a luxury as having a cleaning person come into her home once a week. But for many it is a possibility worth considering. Perhaps you can find a reliable high school student who would work for you at less than the rate of a professional service. It may be possible to trim your budget in some area to free up money for household help. Is it foolish to spend money on a cleaner, or is it worth every penny in the time and energy left over for other things? I have hired house cleaners during especially busy or difficult times and have found it to be well worth the dollars spent.

The third option for help with our work is to team up with friends. Perhaps one mother could watch the other's children while her friend has a day at home alone to give the house a thorough cleaning. The next week they swap roles and the other mom has her day to herself. I have heard of groups of three or four women who designate a day for each of their homes and work together to tackle window washing, spring cleaning, or other major projects. It can be more fun and efficient working as a team.

If we have friends or family who offer to lend a helping hand during difficult times, we need to gracefully welcome their help. Often it is not finances that prohibit recruiting household help but pride! It is hard to admit that we don't get it all done. Let's risk admitting that we can't do it all, all the time, and ask for help!

OBLITERATE COMPARISONS

We tend to play the comparison game in many arenas. Our homes are no exception. We try to keep up with the right furnishings and decorations. We turn into cleaning maniacs when company is coming, going beyond what is reasonable to tackle things people won't likely notice.

When we are working, we berate ourselves for not doing all the things our stay-at-home friends are doing. If we are home full time, we compare ourselves to the working mom who seems to accomplish just as much while putting in many hours outside the home. Many of us are juggling part-time careers and home life, and we aren't sure how to manage it all. Worse yet, we compare our housekeeping to that of our mothers, grandmothers, sisters, and aunts. We may even compare our homes to those we see in the magazines or on television.

What does this get us? A lot of stress and guilt. I am not advocating the elimination of all standards. However, I do recommend that you establish a level of housekeeping that is comfortable for your own family. Most of us can't have perfectly ordered homes without sacrificing time doing other important things. Most of us can't have all the right furnishings without creating financial burden and debt.

Have a family meeting to identify what your standards of housekeeping will be and adjust your desires and schedules accordingly. Let those standards be the only measuring stick you use. Comparing your housekeeping to others' is a losing battle and to continue it will cause great discontent in your home.

MANAGE WELL

"Looks like you're doing a good job!" my husband exclaimed as he found me curled up with a book and a cup of coffee one snowy afternoon. I didn't have the vaguest idea what he was talking about. Just before he responded to the puzzled look on my face, I remembered the title of the book I was reading. Boldly imprinted on the cover were the words *How to Avoid Housework*. This book was one of several in my collection about how to manage a household. Although I work best with structure and schedules, learning to manage my work in the home has been an uphill battle. Being organized and self-disciplined does not come naturally for me. I continually strive to grow and improve in this area.

Teachers turn in lesson plans, business leaders set goals, factory workers meet quotas, and nurses see patients according to a schedule. Why is it that we often run our homes without a plan? Following the maxim "plan your work and work your plan" is as important for the home-maker as it is for any other professional. Most of us don't need to work harder; we need to work smarter. We can better manage our work as we practice the following.

Make a daily schedule. This can be as detailed or as sim-ple as you'd like, but have some plan as to what you will accomplish that day. Keep in mind that there will be inter-ruptions, especially with children in the home. Prioritize your list so the most important or the most difficult jobs are done first. Schedule jobs requiring a lot of energy at a time when you are at your best.

Record your accomplishments. Checking off items on your "to do" list is a good feeling. Remember to focus on what you accomplish and not on what you don't.

Simplify your life. Keep close check on your outside activities and make sure you are doing only those things that you feel God would want you to do. His plans for you will also be compatible with taking care of your family. Just as we have a "to do" list, we must also maintain a "not to do" list. These lists change from one stage of life to another. With growing families, we need to reevaluate from time to time.

De-clutter. Is your *stuff* taking over your *life?* If something is not useful or beautiful, get rid of it. A few years ago, I did some de-cluttering in our home. I found myself dusting furniture that wasn't useful and fussing with bric-a-brac that did nothing for the décor. After putting away many of the things cluttering our rooms, I was surprised that no one in my family noticed they were missing. Rather than looking bare, the rooms looked better with the few special pieces I kept.

I also noticed I was washing clothes seldom worn that somehow found their way into the hampers. It was difficult to put away clothes in our small closets and limited drawer space because they were filled with outdated items. It was amazing how much room we had once I cleared them out. It was also easier to face the chore of putting away laundry when it was no longer a wrestling match with the closet door.

Find new methods. Spend an afternoon at a bookstore or the library to research some home-management methods. Don't be afraid to pick and choose by implementing what works for you and discarding what does not suit you. Take small steps, adding only one new idea at a time.

ESCAPE OCCASIONALLY

As the old McDonald's ad said, "You deserve a break today!" (Nevertheless, to the mother of young children, the ball pit at the Golden Arches might not be a place of refreshment!) We are often reminded to take time out for ourselves, but we seldom practice this principle. It is important to make time to rest and relax if you want to be a homemaker for the long run and not just the short sprint.

Occasionally, you need to be physically removed from your work environment. This can be tricky when your workplace is also your home. Getting away from home, even for an evening, can be one of the most refreshing things you can do. Here are some other ideas:

◆ *Plan breaks within your workday.* If you were in a job outside your home, you would likely have a scheduled time when you would take a coffee break or a lunch hour. Give yourself that same privilege at home. Mothers often resist taking a break when their children are napping. Considering that most women at home—or in the workplace—are putting in a long day from breakfast to dinner dishes, this is definitely false guilt. Taking a midday break will conserve energy for the evening rush.

◆ *Plan a quitting time.* It is the nature of housework to never really be done. We need to set a time that we are going to quit for the evening and stick to it. When you have young children, you often aren't off duty until they are tucked in for the night. Hopefully, you can put an end to the other chores before then. It often seems that moms never get to sit down. Sometimes that is more our own choosing than necessity.

◆ *Nurture your relationship with God.* One of the most common complaints from Christian women raising families is that it is impossible to find time for prayer and Bible reading. It is true that this stage of life is difficult, and it is important to set realistic goals. However, the same time pressures also affect college students, business leaders, even retirees who find themselves busy with traveling or caring for grandchildren and aging parents. The reality is we make time for what is important to us. There will always be distractions to draw us away from that essential time with God.

Your Home, a Sanctuary

There is so much more that could be written about the home front. Loving our families at home involves a lot more than doing dishes and laundry. Our homes are to be sanctuaries of love and acceptance, greenhouses for spiritual growth, and a welcoming oasis for guests who might need a warm bed or a hot cup of coffee. I have chosen to address the daily grind of housework because, for me at least, this has been the most stressful bit. When I am at peace about how my home is running, I have the resources to offer all the rest to those who pass over our threshold.

By God's grace, I have come a long way from being the depressed, stressed-out woman I described earlier. I am no longer grieving the loss of the fairy tale. I accept that my home, my children, and my life will never be perfect. There are still days when I get behind in housework and feel out of control, but instead of feeling ashamed and like a failure, I rally the troops, assign chores, and get things sorted out. I still pray for self-discipline and seek ways to improve my home-management skills. But I no longer base my self-worth on my performance. When things are going well, I thank God for His help in the tasks. If I know that I have been neglectful of my home, I confess my sin and take action to correct things. If there are circumstances beyond my control creating the problem, I accept that life is just that way sometimes. Best of all, I understand that God's love and acceptance never fail, even if I fall short of a goal.

As with many things in life, we need to aim for God's best but accept His love and grace in areas of weakness. We must learn to be patient with ourselves as we grow. With God's help, we can become the unique women that He intended. I pray that your home reflects God's peace, love, and the individuality of your family.

DIGGING DEEPER

1. Check the phrase that best describes how you immediately feel when you consider the task of caring for your home.
   ☐ Overwhelmed
   ☐ Excited at the possibilities
   ☐ That things are going well
   ☐ Angry and frustrated
   ☐ A sense of failure
   ☐ Other: _____

2. Read Genesis 2:15 and Genesis 3:17-19. How did Adam's work change after the Fall?

   Why do you think God included work in Adam's daily life even in idyllic Eden?

3. Look up the following verses and identify some of the consequences of neglecting work.
   Proverbs 10:4

   Proverbs 19:15

2 Thessalonians 3:10

4. Read the story of Mary and Martha in Luke 10:38-42 and compare the behavior of these two sisters. How did Jesus respond to each of them?

5. Consider the following verses and identify some attitudes and actions that reflect a biblical work ethic. Proverbs 14:1

Ephesians 6:7

Colossians 3:23-24

1 Timothy 5:14

6. Assess your homemaking style by marking an X anywhere on the line below:

| Fanatically clean | Tidy but "lived in" | Complete mayhem |

Are you and your family members content with the level of comfort in your home? If not, where would you like it to be on this graph, and how might you get there?

7. This chapter included four tips for homemakers: ask for help, obliterate comparisons, manage well, and escape occasionally. Which of these is most difficult for you? How will you attempt to improve in this area?

8. Invite an older or more experienced woman to lunch. Discuss the following with her:
   ◆ What do you find most difficult about homemaking?
   ◆ How have you overcome your struggles?
   ◆ How do you balance home and career?
   ◆ What advice can you offer to someone who struggles with _____ (your personal struggle here) in relation to homemaking?
   ◆ What have been some of the rewards of your years of work in your home?

Chapter Seven

DELIBERATE ACTS OF KINDNESS

Showing God's Love to Others

BY PAM MILLER

Then [the older women] can train the younger women . . . to be kind.

Titus 2:4-5

I f you simply read the newspaper and watched the evening news, you would be convinced of two things: that the world is not a safe place and people are evil. You would conclude that people don't care about others and that kindness hardly exists. Scan a few headlines from a morning paper:

- ◆ Luggage explodes in bus, killing 26.
- ◆ Date-rape drug case results in guilty plea.
- ◆ Three teens killed in drive-by shooting.
- ◆ Hotel operator admits to pool violation in boy's drowning.

Whether you believe people are basically good or basically evil, you have to agree with one thing: God did not intend our world to be the way it is.

The apostle Paul encouraged women to learn kindness—the antithesis of what we see in our world today. But many factors hinder kindness in our society. Let's look at some of the most prominent ones: violence, selfishness, busyness, and our own hearts.

Violence. This, of course, is not just a problem in slums and seedy parts of town. Violence is rampant in suburbs, upper-income neighborhoods, prestigious schools, and everywhere else. We live in a culture of violence and are bombarded by cruel and aggressive attitudes and actions in music, video games, movies, on Internet sites, and on television. In 1998, the average American consumed 11.8 hours of media daily. By the age of eighteen, the average American child sees 200,000 violent acts on television; 16,000 of them are murders.[1] Violent images penetrating our minds can desensitize us to real-life brutality and numb us to people and their needs.

Selfishness. The current magazine titles *Me, Self,* and *All About You!* reveal our society's priorities. We are consumed with our needs and obsessed with our looks, image, and status. The disregard for others and the focus on self are exemplified by the slogans "If it feels good, do it!" "Look out for number one!" and the bumper sticker I recently saw, "It's all about ME." When our eyes are on ourselves, we don't see others and their needs clearly.

Busyness. The convenience of the Internet saves us time. Now we can buy groceries, rent videos, take college courses, and buy airline tickets and other products online. E-mail helps us keep in touch with family and friends and discuss business with coworkers. Being able to "pay at the pump" with your credit card is wonderful, especially if you are in a hurry. While these services are convenient, they can also cause us to lose the ability to connect with others face to face.

Our busy lifestyles, too, can cause us to become detached from people. This leads to becoming impersonal and indifferent to people because we fail to connect with them. When time is our scarcest resource, reaching out in kindness to others is not uppermost in our minds.

"In a fast-food culture," a wise Benedictine monk observed, "you have to remind yourself that some things cannot be done quickly."[2] Simply put, kindness takes time.

Our own hearts. Romans 3:23 and Jeremiah 17:9 tell us we are all sinners with deceitful hearts. Our natural tendency is to be selfish, caring primarily about ourselves. If this attitude persists, our hearts will begin to harden and we'll become insensitive to people and their needs.

The story in Luke 16:19-25 illustrates the outcome of an insensitive and cold heart. Luke writes of a rich man who had it all—fine clothes and luxury. A beggar named Lazarus, starving and covered in sores, was lying by the rich man's gate. All Lazarus wanted from the rich man was the food that fell from his table. But the rich man chose to ignore Lazarus and his needs.

Later, both men died. The rich man, now in hell, looked up and saw Lazarus by Abraham's side in heaven. The rich man begged Abraham to have pity on him and wanted Lazarus to dip the tip of his finger in water and cool his tongue, for he was in agony. "But Abraham replied, 'Son, remember that in your lifetime you received your good things, while Lazarus received bad things, but now he is comforted here and you are in agony'" (Luke 16:25).

Author Leslie Flynn offers this insight: "The great crime of the rich man, as Jesus told the story, was his failure to respond to the pleas of Lazarus for food. *The rich man's heart was not moved with pity,* though he could see and hear the beggar who was at his gate every day."[3]

When Jesus encountered insensitivity to people's needs, He became angry. In Mark 3, the Pharisees opposed Jesus healing a man on the Sabbath. This was an opportunity to accuse Jesus rather than rejoice with Him. Mark tells us that Jesus "looked around at them in anger and [was] deeply distressed at their stubborn hearts" (verse 5). The Pharisees didn't care about this sick man because their hearts were hardened.

The Heart of Kindness

How can we develop a heart of kindness? In Luke 10:27 Jesus tells us, "'Love the Lord your God with all your heart and with all your soul and with all your strength and with all your mind'; and 'Love your neighbor as yourself.'" Our priorities need to be adjusted so that they will reflect this command of Jesus. When our eyes are on Jesus and loving Him wholeheartedly, the love of Christ will control us (see 2 Corinthians 5:14). His love will impact our lives, softening our hearts toward others and their needs.

John 15:5-10 provides a couple of keys to living this out. "I am the vine; you are the branches," Jesus said. "If a man remains in me and I in him, he will bear much fruit; apart from me you can do nothing" (verse 5). The phrase "remains in me" implies a close relationship with Jesus — continuous fellowship with Him. Just as branches need to be connected to the vine to develop and bear fruit, so we need to be connected to Jesus in order to love the way He does. Verse 10 indicates another key to loving this way: "If you obey my commands, you will remain in my love, just as I have obeyed my Father's commands and remain in his love." Obeying God's Word is *essential* for abiding with Jesus and reflecting His heart toward others.

Galatians 5:22-23 lists the fruit of the Holy Spirit that will grow in your life as you abide in Christ: "The fruit of the Spirit is love, joy, peace, patience, kindness, goodness, faithfulness, gentleness and self-control." As you obey God's Word and draw closer to Jesus daily, fruit bearing will be the result. Abiding with Jesus will transform your heart toward others, causing you to love your neighbor as yourself.

Kindness in Action

Once our hearts are transformed by Jesus' love, our desire will be to reach out and touch others through acts of kindness.

I had been praying for Susan, a secretary I worked with, for many months. Susan was struggling with financial problems, a marital separation, and her daughter's sickness. On several occasions, I stopped by Susan's desk to ask how she was. Susan sensed I cared and soon opened up and shared her struggles with me. Listening to her pain often brought tears to my eyes.

Sensing God's prompting, I picked up a few carnations and enclosed an encouraging note to Susan. She was deeply touched and told me how much this gift meant. Except for Secretary's Day, *no one* had ever given her flowers. Soon after, Susan's heart softened toward God and she accompanied me to church. God is continuing to draw Susan to Himself.

A sacrificial act that impacted the course of my life occurred shortly after I met Kevin, who later became my husband. There was a certain specialness about Kevin that made me feel he might be "the one." Having gone home to Ohio for Thanksgiving, I was telling my grandparents about Kevin. They were excited about the possibility that this relationship could evolve into marriage. At the same time, I also told them about my financial struggles and that I needed to get a second job. Being concerned that this would hinder a potential relationship, my grandparents wrote out a check to cover my outstanding credit card debt so I wouldn't have to work two jobs. I was flabbergasted!

My grandparents' kind act allowed Kevin and me to continue to spend time together—and two months later, we were engaged! Kevin and I will always be grateful for my grandparents' "kindness in action."

Many times, an act of kindness like this takes just a few moments, but that small act can impact a person for a lifetime. It was Mother Teresa who said, "We cannot do great things—only small things with great love."

LISTENING

Listening is one of the highest compliments we can give to another, because it communicates care, acceptance, and love. Consider this story:

> Mamie Adams always went to a branch post office in her town because the postal employees were friendly. She went there to buy stamps just before Christmas one year and the lines were particularly long. Someone pointed out that there was no need to wait in line because there was a stamp machine in the lobby. "I know," said Mamie, "but the machine won't ask me about my arthritis."[4]

For Mamie, having contact with kind people far outweighed the benefit of saved time.

ENCOURAGEMENT

Solomon said in Proverbs 25:11, "A word aptly spoken is like apples of gold in settings of silver." Kindness can also come in the form of "words aptly spoken," such as words of encouragement. As Mother Teresa said, "Kind words can be short and easy to speak, but their echoes are endless."

We need to ask God to help us to be sensitive to others' need for encouragement. We need to listen for clues in what people say. We need to obey God's leading when He nudges our hearts to encourage others. It is probably just what they need at the time.

As authors Jerry and Mary White say, "Encouragement can provide increased self-esteem, a brighter outlook on life, more positive thinking, and spiritual uplifting."[5] Don't keep those kind words to yourself! Speak up and share them! The impact will be felt greatly.

KINDNESS TO FAMILY

When kindness pervades your home, it becomes a peaceful sanctuary. Unfortunately, it often seems easier to be kinder to strangers than to family. Perhaps we set standards and expectations too high for those we love. When our loved ones do not meet our expectations, we get hurt and retaliate. Kindness does not take any more time and effort than other reactions, yet it pays unbelievable dividends!

In his book *Secret Choices*, Dr. Ed Wheat stresses that private decisions we make in our family relationships will determine the quality of those relationships. We choose to react to others' behavior. One choice may not be major, but a series of positive or negative choices leaves a mark.

> Though our choices are small when counted one at a time, their cumulative effect is more powerful than we can imagine. In reality, these private choices direct our steps, determine our behavior, change the quality of our relationships, and in the end, shape our lives.[6]

Are your secret choices moving you toward successful

relationships? Determine to choose kind attitudes, words, and deeds when relating to your spouse and children. Over time, these consistently kind acts will create loving and gracious interactions.

Another way to show kindness to others is to consider their needs above your own, as Philippians 2:3-4 says. Ask the Lord to help you slow down so you can see what your husband or children need. Praying for them will also keep your heart kind and soft toward them. Not only will they benefit from your prayers, but so will you, as kind words and kind deeds flow from a kind heart.

Treating your family with kindness will have one other important result: it will provide an example for your children. Early on, children look to their parents for cues on how to respond to life events. As someone has said, "Children are a great deal more apt to follow your lead than the way you point."

Once I read a story about a family eating dinner in a restaurant. During the meal, the youngest daughter knocked over her glass of milk. The mother, without any disapproval in her voice, gently said, "It's okay, honey. We'll help you clean it up." Then every family member grabbed napkins and wiped up the spill.

Ever been there? What is your normal reaction to a possibly chaotic scene such as this? Do you start yelling, blaming, shaming, or making a scene?

Think of the impact the mother's response had on the daughter and the other siblings! What this mother taught was the heart of kindness—the ability to respond in a positive way to a bad situation, and that it's okay to make mistakes. When accidents occur, everyone needs to pitch in and help. The mother taught all this by *modeling* kindness.

Our children imitate not only our actions, but also our attitudes. That is why an attitude of kindness and cheerful servanthood is important. Tricia Goyer wrote, "We all try to do nice things for our spouses and children. But even more important than what we do is how we act. The difference between 'doing things' and 'serving others' is a matter of attitude."[7]

What type of attitude do you have when you cook dinner or fold laundry? How do you feel about serving your family? Are you joyful or resentful? My friend Beth prays for each family member as she folds that person's clothing. Wouldn't that change your attitude toward this "chore" quickly?

Goyer also wrote, "If we want our children to willingly reach out to others and show kindness and compassion, it's essential that they see us do the same."[8] This is exactly what Albert Schweitzer, 1952 Nobel Peace Prize winner, meant when he said, "Example is not the main thing in influencing others. It is the only thing."[9]

KINDNESS TO NEIGHBORS

Ann Kiemel's book *I'm Out to Change My World* impacted me greatly as a young Christian. Reading the book broadened my concept of whom God wanted me to reach. I was challenged by how simply Ann shared Jesus' love with her neighbors. Ann prayed for her neighbors, talked and listened to them, and went out of her way to be kind to them—all so they would be touched by Jesus' love. Ann cared about her neighbors, and her actions and words demonstrated it.

The people who live the closest to us are the ones we can so easily overlook. God has *you* in your neighborhood for a reason. It may be just to touch one lost soul.

I learned a huge lesson about this. Being busy with my full-time job in youth ministry, I did not get acquainted with my neighbors. Knowing we were moving soon to another East Peoria neighborhood, I was sad I had not taken the time to reach out. I asked God to forgive me for neglecting those He had placed around me, and then prayed that He would use me to share His love and kindness with my new neighbors. I knew I'd still be busy, but this time I wanted to *make* the time to reach out.

After we moved, I delivered chocolate chip cookies (an "Ann Kiemel tradition") to each household, letting them know I was glad to be their neighbor and was looking forward to getting to know them.

It's been exciting to see what God has done with my prayer and willingness to be used by Him in my neighborhood. I have hosted a 5-Day Club in the summer for many years, a ministry of Child Evangelism Fellowship that includes fun times of Bible stories, songs, memorization, and games. Several of the children who come do not regularly attend church, and it has been thrilling to introduce them to Christ. In fact, one little girl referred to 5-Day Club as "going to church at Pam's." Numerous children have made a decision to receive Christ as their personal Savior through this outreach.

Every December I have a Christmas caroling party for the neighborhood children. It's a wonderful evening of fun, which ends with a birthday cake to celebrate Jesus' birth. After one of these parties, a neighbor wrote me a thank-you note that said, "Your family is a *joy* to our neighborhood." What an encouragement to keep showing kindness to my neighbors!

KINDNESS TO STRANGERS

Has a stranger ever dropped money in your parking meter so you wouldn't get a ticket? Have you ever been surprised when a stranger gave you and your child her extra Chuck E. Cheese's tickets? If something like this has happened to you, it surely brought a smile to your face!

One morning in Portland, Oregon, the owner of a drive-through coffee business was surprised when a customer paid not only for her own mocha, but also for the coffee for the person in the car behind her. The owner loved being able to tell the next customer her drink had already been paid for. The second customer was so pleased that she purchased the coffee for the customer behind *her*. This kind act had a ripple effect that lasted two hours as people kept buying coffees and lattes for others. In the end, it made a strong impression on *twenty-seven* customers![10]

Imagine how much this world would be affected if each of us performed one act of kindness a week and the recipient of our kindness passed it on. It could change the atmosphere of public places!

Here are some other ideas to get you started in showing kindness to strangers:

◆ If you notice the cashier has had a rough day, buy her a candy bar.

◆ Surprise the mail carrier or trash collector with a plate of cookies, lemonade, or a thank-you note.

◆ Offer your seat on a crowded bus or train.

◆ Pay the toll of the driver behind you.

◆ Hold the door open for others.

◆ Mow your neighbors' yard or shovel their driveway.

◆ Bring your shopping cart back to the front of the store.

◆ Pick up litter.

◆ Let someone go ahead of you in the grocery store if he or she has fewer items than you do.

◆ Surprise someone at work with a cup of coffee or soda.

As Dale Carnegie once said, "Be kind, for everyone you meet is fighting a battle." We need to remember that others, too, have feelings, families, and hectic schedules.

Being kind shows that you value them.

Don't forget to apply these principles of kindness to the newcomers in your church. Make them feel welcome! Ask them out to lunch or over to your house for dessert and coffee. Keep in mind how *you* felt when you visited your church for the first time. Who reached out to you? Pass that same kindness on!

KINDNESS TO "THE LEAST OF THESE"

As I have mentioned, kindness does not happen naturally. We need to be intentional about showing kindness, particularly to those outside our comfort zone. Jesus commands us to do just that:

> "'For I was hungry and you gave me something to eat, I was thirsty and you gave me something to drink, I was a stranger and you invited me in, I needed clothes and you clothed me, I was sick and you looked after me, I was in prison and you came to visit me.'
>
> "Then the righteous will answer him, 'Lord, when did we see you hungry and feed you, or thirsty and give you something to drink? When did we see you a stranger and invite you in, or needing clothes and clothe you? When did we see you sick or in prison and go to visit you?'
>
> "The King will reply, 'I tell you the truth, whatever you did for one of *the least of these* brothers of mine, you did for me.'" (Matthew 25:35-40, emphasis added)

Jesus' command is for us to reach out to the hungry, thirsty, poor, strangers, and prisoners. We are not to close our hearts toward them, but to be open for God to use us. We need to remember that God created everyone in His image and that He loves us all very much.

Rush Yarnell is an example of a real-life Good Samaritan. One evening in January 1994, during rush hour, Rush just happened to see in his rearview mirror a small boy collapse onto the snow-covered sidewalk. It was one of Detroit's coldest days, with a wind chill of fifty degrees below zero.

Without thinking twice, Rush crossed four lanes of traffic and made two U-turns before stopping in the middle of the street. With car horns honking and motorists shouting, Rush ran and picked up the unconscious boy and brought him back to his car. He thought the little boy was dead.

Rush took nine-year-old Darrin to the nearest police station, and the police immediately transported him to the hospital. After eight days in the hospital, Darrin made a full recovery. But the story does not stop here, as Rush's heart was touched by this boy. He bought Darrin a color television, complete with Nintendo games — on the condition that Darrin would spend as much time studying as he did playing.

Rush's act of kindness made a significant impact on Darrin's life. Darrin's grades went from Ds and Fs to As and Bs.[11] Darrin will never be the same because of Rush's obedience to Jesus' command in Matthew 25.

Closer to home, in Peoria, Illinois, where I live, a ministry called Sidewalk Sunday School reaches at-risk children who are unchurched and in desperate need of love. Many times this ministry targets high-crime areas where there are needy children. When the volunteers go into these neighborhoods and set up the stage, sound system, and supplies, the children soak up the love of Jesus and His Word.

When asked about the possible danger of being in these high-crime areas, the director, Jan, states, "I would rather be in these risky areas *in* God's will than be at home in my own bed *out* of God's will."

James wrote, "Suppose a brother or sister is without clothes and daily food. If one of you says to him, 'Go, I wish you well; keep warm and well fed,' but does nothing about his physical needs, what good is it? In the same way, faith by itself, if it is not accompanied by action, is dead" (2:15-17). God's Word is clear that He wants you to have a kind heart toward the poor and to respond when given the opportunity. Allow God to use you to meet others' needs.

The Ultimate Expression of Kindness

God showed us the ultimate expression of kindness through His Son. Titus 3:4 says, "But when the kindness and love of God our Savior appeared, he saved us."

Not only did God in His kindness give us His Son and salvation, but He also gave us "everything we need for life and godliness" and "his very great and precious promises" (2 Peter 1:3-4). What more could you ask for?

God's kindness can be shared with others in two powerful ways: actions and words.

Actions. Matthew 5:16 tells us: "Let your light shine before men, that they may see your good deeds and praise your Father in heaven." Your life needs to communicate loud and clear that there is something *different* about you. As people get closer to you, that difference should stand out even more. Romans 12:2 reminds us that a Christian's life and values should be contrary to the world's. If we are being obedient to the Word by being kind, we will stand out like a light in the darkness.

People will also notice a difference in your life when your priorities are in order. The best recipe for **JOY** is to put **J**esus first, **O**thers second, and **Y**ourself last in your life. This **JOY** will shine brightly in our dark world.

Words. You can share God's kindness through *words*. Your personal testimony of how God has shown His kindness to you is effective because it's *your* story and no one can refute it. Allowing others to hear about God's love and kindness in your life will intrigue them; they will want to know more. When others begin to ask questions, what will you say? We are to be ready at all times to share about Christ with others, according to 1 Peter 3:15.

If you are unsure how to share the gospel, seek out an "older" Christian woman for instruction. Don't forget you are God's messenger of His good news (see Romans 10:14), and take that responsibility seriously. God's Word is clear in 1 John 5:11-12 that only those who have received Jesus as their personal Savior will spend eternity in heaven. Thus, the ultimate expression of kindness is to share the gospel.

When you have "tasted the kindness of the Lord" (1 Peter 2:3, NASB), your natural response is to pass it on to others. Don't keep the good news to yourself! *Be kind* and share it with others!

DIGGING DEEPER

1. How would you define kindness?

2. Name some of the cultural influences that may be distracting you from others' needs (such as busyness or watching too much television).

3. Contrast today's cultural influences with what the following Scriptures say.
Romans 8:6-8

Philippians 4:8

Colossians 3:1-2

4. What kind act(s) did Jesus perform in each of these passages?
Mark 6:34-44

Luke 8:43-48

John 8:1-11

Titus 3:4-6

5. From the following Scriptures, identify ways you can show kindness.
   Matthew 5:43-44

   Ephesians 4:32

   Hebrews 3:13

   James 1:19

   James 2:15-17

   1 Peter 3:15

6. Describe the attitude you need to have toward others according to the following verses.
   John 15:12

   Romans 10:1

Philippians 2:3-5

James 2:1-9

7. What is one act of kindness someone did for you that you will never forget?

8. What is one act of kindness *you* can do during the next week?

9. How is your attitude toward serving others? Joyful or resentful? What are some ways you can create a more joyful, kind heart toward others?

10. According to Proverbs 23:7, "As he thinks within himself, so he is" (NASB). Why do you need to be careful about what you put in your mind?

Chapter Eight

SUBMIT, WHO ME?

Responding to Authority

BY SANDY KERSHAW

Then [the older women] can train the younger
women . . . to be subject to their husbands.

Titus 2:4-5

The tides move in and out. The Moon revolves
around the Earth. Seasons come and go. Plants
grow from seed; then they flower, wither, and die.
People are born, grow, mature, become old, and die. It is
the natural progression of things.

We only need to read the account of Creation in
Scripture—or study life cycles and food chains in biol-
ogy—to understand that God has given us order. As
stated by Solomon in Ecclesiastes, there is a time for everything under heaven (3:1).

When the Israelites' concerns were beginning to overwhelm Moses, his father-in-law, Jethro, suggested that
Moses appoint judges to decide simple cases, saving the
difficult ones for Moses. "That will make your load

lighter," Jethro said, ". . . you will be able to stand the strain" (Exodus 18:22-23).

There was then an *order and line of authority* in managing the Israelites, similar to the one America's founding fathers set up for us in the Constitution. Every state has its officials to run state business. Every city, town, and village has leaders to handle its business. Order and authority are absolutely essential for our world to run efficiently and smoothly.

So, too, with relationships: Not everyone can be the leader. Likewise, someone who is a leader in one group will not necessarily be a leader in a different group. Therefore, when there is a line of authority, there must also be submission: deference to the decisions of another person.

In New Testament Greek, the word translated *submit* is *hupotasso*. *Hupo* means "under" and *tasso* means "to voluntarily complete, arrange, adapt, or blend so as to make a complete whole." It was primarily used as a military term meaning to fill each vacancy in a legion so that every rank of the formation is in a chain of authority, complete, at full strength, and ready to do battle.[1]

In God's army, the smallest battle unit is the family, and the leader of this unit is your husband. The apostle Paul is clear in his letter to Titus that women are "to be subject to [that is, to submit to] their husbands." You and your children fall under his authority so that your unit can operate at full strength and effectiveness.

Other examples show that submission is at the heart of God's ordered world. When Jesus walked the Earth as a man, He continually submitted to His Father's will. Thirty-five times in the book of John, Jesus refers to the Father "who sent me." Christ came to Earth to do the will of the Father—He submitted completely. Christ is our model of submission. He is not asking us to do something He hasn't done. Nor is He asking us to do something He won't help us do. Likewise, the Holy Spirit submits to the wishes of the Son in teaching, guiding, and comforting believers. In order to line up under God's authority, we need to understand His view.

Perhaps the best way to consider submission is to start with the instruction found in Romans 12:2: "Do not conform any longer to the pattern of this world, but be transformed by the renewing of your mind." As Christ-followers we have a new way of viewing life because we look to His Word to direct us. This is how we renew our minds. We no longer let the ideas and opinions of worldly people dictate our thoughts and actions.

The world would have us believe that:

◆ Submission means to become a slave.
◆ Submission means to be inferior.
◆ Submission refers to keeping women as doormats to be walked on and taken advantage of by their husbands.
◆ Submission is a negative, ugly word that is no longer applicable to women.

Keep in mind that submission in God's plan has to do with position, not worth. Men and women are *equal* in the following ways:

◆ They are both created by God.
◆ They are both made in God's image.
◆ They are equally called to obedience and responsibility.
◆ They are equally sinful and recipients of God's grace.

Though men and women are the same in many respects, in God's order they do differ in their responsibilities.[2]

A woman may be the CEO of a prosperous company, a skilled defense attorney, an accountant, a surgeon, or a manager that wields power and authority over men and women alike. But in family matters, her husband holds the main leadership responsibilities. Submission is an attitude of the heart, an attitude of yieldedness and love.

When we renew our minds by replacing what the world says with what God's Word says, we will understand submission as God intended. Then, as the rest of Romans 12:2 tells us, we "will be able to test and approve what God's will is—his good, pleasing and perfect will." Doing that perfect will is our ultimate goal.

When we keep this goal uppermost in our minds, submitting to any authority becomes much easier.

The Bible Says That?

Scripture says all women believers are to submit, and they are to submit as follows:

- ◆ To God (James 4:7)
- ◆ To rulers (Hebrews 13:17; 1 Peter 2:13)
- ◆ To their own husbands (Titus 2:5; 1 Peter 3:1-2)
- ◆ To each other (Ephesians 5:21)

Our verse in Titus refers specifically to wives submitting to their husbands, so that is the focus of this chapter. But to fully understand how a wife can do this, we first need to understand what it means to submit to Christ, for submission to our husbands comes from our submission to the Lord. We place ourselves under Christ's authority and surrender our thoughts and actions to His leading. What does He want us to do? Love Him, trust Him, and obey His Word.

Paul tells us in 2 Corinthians 10:5 that we should

"take captive every thought to make it obedient to Christ." We are to tune out the messages of the world. If we don't take erroneous thoughts captive and replace them with truth, we will struggle with Paul's directive in Titus. As we dwell on truth and abide in Christ (see John 15:7), submission will become easier. He has even equipped us with the power to submit: "for it is God who works in you to will and to act according to his good purpose" (Philippians 2:13).

Submit to My Husband? You're Kidding, Right?

As I mentioned previously, God has a divine order for the family. The man is the head of the wife (see 1 Corinthians 11:3). This means that the accountability for decisions concerning the home and family rests with the man.

This headship includes more than just decision making. Paul exhorts husbands to love their wives sacrificially, as Christ loves the church (see Ephesians 5:25-27). They are to love their wives as their own bodies. Husbands should nourish and provide for their wives and deem them as valuable as themselves. Later Paul warns fathers against frustrating their children (see Ephesians 6:4). They are commanded to bring them up in the training and instruction of the Lord. Therefore, the husband is also responsible for providing an atmosphere of love and safety in the home. This is God's plan and loving provision for women and children.

A husband will stand before God one day and answer for his leadership. What an awesome responsibility—one I will gladly allow my husband to have!

Biblically, the wife is the husband's helper. She completes her husband. Her responsibilities include loving her husband (as Titus 2 previously mentioned), respecting her husband (see Ephesians 5:33), and submitting to his authority.

Viewed through the eyes of love and respect, submission is not the harsh, cold, subservient act some women perceive it to be. Out of this love and loyalty to our husbands we will defer to their decisions, but God intends for us to help in the decision-making process.

Mothers who are home full time are the greatest sources of information about the home and family because that's where their focus is. They know their children's trials, fears, accomplishments, struggles, and myriad other subjects that pertain to their family life. Mothers who work outside the home are still responsible to provide pertinent information to their husbands, although their focus is divided between job and home.

I was home when our children were young so I knew firsthand the problems, activities, and situations of their lives. I knew what our schedules could handle. I had my finger on the pulse of our family. Steve, on the other hand, was away all day. His focus was on his job. The briefings I would give him about family matters became even more important when he began traveling. During those times, most home decisions were made by me, sometimes after discussing them with Steve when he called. However, the information wives share is not limited to only the home and children. Whether it's financial decisions, vacation plans, job changes, or other major decisions that affect the marriage and family, wives are to offer their perspectives and wisdom.

In order for a husband to make wise, well-informed decisions, he should look to his wife to give as much input as possible on a subject before deciding. Steve defers many decisions to me, but *he* will be accountable to God for that decision. *I* will be accountable to God for submitting to my husband's decision as well as for the decisions I make. Men might not know that they should listen to their wives. Don't hold back simply because your husband doesn't ask for information. Share your thoughts and ideas with him—but in a loving, non-controlling manner. Your attitude will be most important. If we develop the "gentle and quiet spirit" spoken of in 1 Peter 3:3-5, we will be able to present a non-hostile, non-combative, non-domineering attitude to decisions our husbands make.

Many women fear submission. They wrongly believe it means they will be controlled and enslaved. The truth is that biblical submission gives them freedom.

A book called *The Surrendered Wife* by Laura Doyle encourages women to relinquish control to their husbands. Though her book is not written from a Christian perspective, Doyle hits the bull's-eye when she says:

> Surrendering to your husband is not about returning to the fifties or rebelling against feminism. This book isn't about dumbing down or being rigid. It's certainly not about subservience. . . . It's about having a relationship that brings out the best in both of you, and growing together as spiritual beings.[3]

Me—A Doormat?

So am I a doormat, stepped on and taken advantage of? No. I hold serious responsibilities of my own in sharing my insights, opinions, facts, and intuition with Steve. But what if I don't agree with his final decision? What if I strongly oppose his choice? I can tell him so, but in a kind and loving manner. (That's sometimes difficult!) Then I'm to stand behind his decision and support him. I give my qualms and misgivings to God.

When Kristin was five and Jeff only ten months old, Steve suggested we spend a week of vacation at a family Bible retreat center in Minnesota. There would be many speakers for the adults and programs for the children.

I didn't want to go. I wasn't going to leave Jeff in the nursery all day and hire sitters for him and Kristin every night. That meant that there would be many activities for adults that Steve and I wouldn't be able to participate in because our children were young.

Steve thought the retreat was a great idea. We discussed my reservations and objections, but he made the decision that we should try it.

I prayed diligently about every detail: room accommodations, meals, seminar sessions, the nursery, spare time, sitters, and on and on. My attitude was first on my prayer list. When it came time to go, I actually had peace about the trip. It still wasn't something that I would have chosen for our vacation, but I was excited about going.

We arrived and checked in to find that most of the conference activities would require Jeff and Kristin to be left in the child-care facilities or with a baby-sitter. Steve was not happy about that. In fact, he was ready to leave! Driving to the apartment assigned to us, he told me he had made a big mistake. The words "I told you so" never entered my mind. Instead I found myself pointing out the positives and suggesting how we could handle the week. This was definitely God working in me! The week was not terrible, but not one we would repeat with young children. We attended several sessions, but spent most of our time alone doing activities our children could also enjoy. Steve's decision might not have been the best, but God brought good out of it.

What would have happened if I hadn't trusted God and submitted my attitude to Him? First, I would have been angry that Steve booked us to go in spite of my objections. I would have allowed resentment to build. Second, every time he mentioned the trip, I would have reminded him by a look or comment that I was totally against the vacation. Third, my attitude would have caused friction between Steve and me and created a negative atmosphere for Kristin and Jeff. Fourth, when the reality of the situation hit Steve, I would have made sure he knew that *I* had been right and had tried to warn him. That would have been a memorable trip for our children!

Steve deserves some credit for my right response. He listened to my objections and concerns, and he discussed how we could handle them. While his final decision wasn't my first choice, at least I knew he had considered my opinion.

My choice was to accept and support his decision or to make all of us miserable by resenting and fighting it. Happily, I chose the former. With God's help, I submitted to and supported Steve.

Wives and children are under God's umbrella of protection; we are not to take matters into our own hands. If our husbands make mistakes (and they will), God will deal with them and the outcome of their decisions. At the same time, God will take care of our needs.

"That's fine for you," you might say, "but my husband is considering a more serious decision with which I disagree." I understand how you must feel. Three years after that vacation, Steve was offered a fantastic job opportunity. He would have responsibilities to develop business on the East Coast for a West Coast company's expansion. My fear was that the job would require him to spend most of his time away from home. Both Steve and his future boss assured me that extensive travel was not necessary. We drew up a list of pros and cons, we discussed them at length, and we prayed. The more we deliberated, the less peace I felt. The amount of travel continued to bother me.

In spite of my misgivings, Steve accepted the position. I was scared and dismayed, but I had been learning about God's protection for wives and children, so I released the situation to God every time I panicked.

As Steve began traveling I wrote in my journal: "God does not want our family to fall apart. I can depend upon Him to help Kristin, Jeff, and me deal with Steve's absences. Lord, I know I need to support Steve's decision. Help me handle all that it entails. I will trust you with my fears and misgivings. You are a big God."

After two months, Steve quit. He was traveling 90 percent of the time, and he said he didn't want his family growing up without him. He confessed to me that the power and prestige had enticed him. He knew his choice wasn't right for *him*, but he made it anyway.

I was shocked! I never dreamed Steve would return to his former job. Your husband might not do such an about-face, but God is with you no matter what.

Do I Submit to My Unbelieving Husband?

You may be wondering how submission applies if your husband isn't a Christ-follower. Do you *still* submit to his authority?

The answer is yes. Love, respect, and submission to his leadership are still your responsibilities. It's true that a nonChristian husband will not necessarily follow the scriptural principles God gave to husbands, but sometimes we automatically assume that such a man's leadership will be foolish, cruel, or wrong. That's not always the case.

Obviously, God does not want you to submit to something illegal, abusive, or immoral. But if your husband's decision does not violate God's Word, then you should submit with the same attitude as though he were a Christian. By submitting to his authority, you are submitting to God. Moreover, 1 Peter 3:1-2 tells us that a wife's submissive behavior may draw her unbelieving husband to Christ.

Consider Angela's situation. She became a believer a year after marrying Joel. He was not interested in spiritual matters, but he had no objections to Angela's church activities as long as they didn't interfere with their life. Joel held a high-powered position with a major corporation, and that job often required Angela and him to entertain business associates in their home.

Entertaining came easily for Joel, who was outgoing and gregarious. Angela found entertaining daunting. But out of her love for Joel, and knowing how important it was to him, she desired to do her best. Shy and quiet, Angela didn't have many mutual interests with the couples who came over, but she was determined to be a gracious hostess.

She enrolled in cooking classes and read books that helped her develop some creative and appealing ways to serve dinners and plan parties. She learned as much as she could about the guests for each occasion so she would be able to enter into conversations. As she became better acquainted with some of the wives, she grew more comfortable and confident with them. She learned that two of them also were planning to attend the community Bible study class that she was joining in the fall. As time passed, she gained new insights about herself and made some new friends.

Why did she make such an effort to entertain well? She shared her answer with me once: "Because I love my husband, and these occasions were so important to him and his work."

There's another reason, too. "Many times Joel has told me how much he appreciates all my efforts," Angela said. "He knows entertaining like this was not easy for me in the beginning. He still isn't interested in spiritual matters. In fact, he plays golf while I attend church. But I believe that if I continue to be his 'partner' in things that matter to him, God will someday reach him. God has already provided some new friends among these wives and, who knows, I might have a whole new ministry!"

Over time Angela has actually come to enjoy entertaining. Why? Because she looks at it with an attitude of love and service for the man she loves.

Then there is Barbara. Her husband, Matt, also wants nothing to do with church. In fact, he can be belligerent about spiritual matters. Often he will say something derogatory about God in an attempt to upset Barbara.

When their two sons were young, Barbara took them to Sunday school. Matt never objected then, but now that the boys are teenagers he says they can choose for themselves whether or not they go to church. His philosophy is "boys will be boys" and "all boys need to sow their wild oats." Barbara cringes each time he says such things, but she attempts to place the boys in God's hands and to believe that God will take care of them.

But she isn't a doormat. She believes Matt's permissiveness can be harmful to her sons and she realizes they will pay a price for any wrongdoing or foolish behavior. She lets Matt know when she disagrees with him and why. She doesn't attempt to "spiritualize" everything she says—she just tries to be honest.

Interestingly, her boys treat her ideas and opinions with respect. Occasionally they have joined her for church by their own choice, and they began attending the high school youth group. Sometimes they even talk with her about their problems. This has amazed and thrilled Barbara.

Many women would have walked out on a husband like Matt, but Barbara continues to love him and submit to his leading. She attempts to concentrate on his strengths and she continues to pray for his salvation, and she has shed many tears over worries about Matt and the boys. How will her situation turn out? Only God knows, but Barbara is willing to wait and see.

To paraphrase a saying, "You might be the only Jesus your husband ever knows." As you develop godly character and love your husband, his heart might just soften to the things of God. If you're married to an unbelieving husband, enlist friends to pray for both of you. Seek another, more experienced woman who is in the same situation and can offer you advice and encouragement.

If Only . . .

If only all husbands were committed to God's principles and cherished their spouse, then wives would find submission to be a normal part of marriage, not requiring any thought or discussion. Each person would fulfill his or her role. Marriages would reflect God's love and couples would stand firm against the pressures of the world. God's reputation would never be discredited, because all husbands and wives would be perfectly united. Christian marriages would shine with the love of God for all to see.

If only all that were true. In reality, we are fallen, sinful humans who often forget that God's design is best. We buy into being "independent" and maintaining our personal "rights." Crouched in our foxholes, we turn against one another, forgetting who the real enemy is.

Submission as designed by our great Creator was never meant to demean, belittle, or squelch. It was intended to strengthen the family, affirm the responsibilities of husbands and wives, and reflect God's orderly character. If we keep in mind God's purpose, submission becomes not a curse, but a blessing.

DIGGING DEEPER

1. What was your attitude toward submission before reading this chapter? Did your perspective change at all as a result of this chapter? In what way?

2. How would you define submission according to the world's view? According to God's view?

3. Submission has nothing to do with value or equality. How are men and women equal? What is the difference between them concerning submission?

4. Read John 13:3-7. What act is described here?

5. What do the following verses say about submission?
   John 13:15-17

   Romans 12:10

   James 4:7

6. According to 1 Peter 3:1-2, what might result when a Christian wife properly submits to her unbelieving husband?

7. What directive is given in Ephesians 5:22 and Colossians 3:18? How are we told to do this?

8. Why is it important that we understand submission?

9. What do you fear most about submitting to your husband? How can you overcome this fear?

10. What is the result of submission?

THE TITUS 2 WOMAN GROWS UP

. . . and Becomes the Proverbs 31 Lady

BY ANGIE CONRAD, PAM MILLER, TAMMY
EAGAN, SANDY KERSHAW, AND JANET COX

The preceding chapters have been full of practical instruction and counsel—but we also hope you've found lots of encouragement, inspiration, and motivation. We've shared our stories—the joys and struggles of five women like you who have held to their faith and attempted to live out God's directives as given by Paul to Titus. We have made plenty of mistakes (still do), but we have also reaped rewards.

As we look back on the life stages we have experienced, we can see that God has been with us every step of the way, even when we doubted. Indeed, He provides rewards to sustain us when we lose hope or grow weary of following the instructions listed in Titus 2. What's more, He gives us a picture of what the rewards of the mature Titus woman might look like. It turns out she looks very much like the woman described in Proverbs 31:

A wife of noble character who can find? She is worth far more than rubies. Her husband has full confidence in her and lacks nothing of value. She brings him good, not harm, all the days of her life.

She selects wool and flax and works with eager hands. She is like the merchant ships, bringing her food from afar. She gets up while it is still dark; she provides food for her family and portions for her servant girls. She considers a field and buys it; out of her earnings she plants a vineyard.

She sets about her work vigorously; her arms are strong for her tasks. She sees that her trading is profitable, and her lamp does not go out at night. In her hand she holds the distaff and grasps the spindle with her fingers.

She opens her arms to the poor and extends her hands to the needy. When it snows, she has no fear for her household; for all of them are clothed in scarlet. She makes coverings for her bed; she is clothed in fine linen and purple.

Her husband is respected at the city gate, where he takes his seat among the elders of the land. She makes linen garments and sells them, and supplies the merchants with sashes. She is clothed with strength and dignity; she can laugh at the days to come.

She speaks with wisdom, and faithful instruction is on her tongue. She watches over the affairs of her household and does not eat the bread of idleness. Her children arise and call her blessed; her husband also, as he praises her: "Many women do noble things, but you surpass them all." Charm is deceptive, and beauty is fleeting;

but a woman who fears the LORD is to be praised.
Give her the reward she has earned, and let her
works bring her praise at the city gate. (Proverbs
31:10-31)

We see the Proverbs 31 woman—whom we like to call
Mrs. P-31 for short—as the young Titus 2 woman *all
grown up*. If the Titus 2 woman is a work in progress, then
the Proverbs 31 woman is the finished product, the goal to
which we aspire.

We all agree that God often has worked in spite of our
flaws and stubbornness. We are amazed that God could
take our simple prayers and commitment to Him and turn
them into something special.

As "older" women, we see the beginnings of new life
all around us—lives that we have had the pleasure of
touching in some small way. We feel the warmth of God's
love and the thrill of knowing that, in spite of our weaknesses, He has taken every moment committed to Him
and turned them into something bigger than we could
have ever imagined. Through the process of time and
experience, we all can gradually become Mrs. P-31 in our
own unique forms.

God's Plan for Women: Risks and Rewards

Remember Jenny from the Introduction? She was the
woman who sat in church and idealized the lives of other
women. Comparing her own life with theirs, she concluded they had it all together. Of course they didn't—
they had problems and disappointments as well. But they
wore their Sunday smiles and impeccable images, which
led Jenny to conclude that their lives were perfect.

So what if one of those ladies had risked reaching
out to Jenny? What if they could have been honest and

vulnerable with each other? If so, perhaps Jenny's story might look like this . . .

At the end of service, Jenny was thankful when the last chorus was sung and the minister asked the congregation to bow their heads in prayer. It gave her just the opportunity she needed to brush a tear from her eye and compose herself before anyone could notice she'd been struggling. A moment later, she quickly slipped out of the sanctuary with a few nods and good-byes to fellow church members.

Jenny retrieved her daughter from her Sunday school class and made a beeline for the door, but the teacher, Claire, gently grabbed Jenny's elbow.

"Jenny," Claire said hesitantly, "how are you this week?"

"Fine," Jenny replied automatically. "Busy as usual. The kids keep me running."

Jenny hoped that Claire hadn't noticed her misty eyes. Jenny tried her best to keep her head down as she helped her daughter with her sweater.

"Jenny, I was wondering if you would like to come to my house tomorrow evening," Claire ventured. "I'm starting a new small group and inviting a few other women. We'd be really pleased if you would join us. It's very informal—we read some Scripture and pray for each other. Mostly, we will just talk about whatever is on our minds—the crisis of the day."

Jenny was surprised by the invitation. At first, she thought she couldn't possibly attend. One more obligation seemed too much to consider. But something about the concern she saw in Claire's eyes made her decide it would be worth a try. Perhaps she would find some encouragement from a group like that. At this point, she had nothing to lose.

"Sure, I'll come," she said at last. "Thanks for the invitation."

The following evening, it wasn't easy to break away from home. Jenny's husband encouraged her to go, but she wasn't convinced he was altogether happy when their daughter refused to stay in bed and the baby started crying just as Jenny was walking out the front door. In spite of the twinge of guilt, she couldn't help smiling as she hopped in the car and backed down the driveway. The silence was wonderful!

Claire's home was an oasis. With her teenagers out for the evening and her husband traveling, the women had the house to themselves. As Jenny and three other women — Claire, Karen, and Sarah — gathered around the kitchen table, the aroma of fresh-brewed coffee and hot-out-of-the-oven cake made everyone relax. Sarah looked especially tired but told the others there was nowhere else she'd rather be.

Jenny was amazed at what took place that evening. It was as if each of these women, one by one, took off a mask and laid it down on the table. Jenny saw Claire, Sarah, and Karen as she had never seen them before. She was humbled to find that her perceptions of them had been wrong. They had many of the same struggles she did, and some even greater. They, too, wondered how they would manage under the stress. But as Jenny risked laying her own mask aside, she found hope just being among women who could relate to her daily challenges.

As the weeks passed and they continued to meet, each woman reaped numerous rewards from their time together. Their friendships grew as they shared joys and sorrows. They enjoyed the freedom of being themselves, not hiding the flaws. They saw their prayers answered, and they waited together for God's solutions to some ongoing problems. Through it all, they changed, even though some circumstances didn't. They became more at peace with themselves and each other. They were released from their own hurts as they sought to heal the wounds of one another. They felt God's pleasure as they gathered each week, drawing closer to Him.

As with Jenny and her group, the five of us have experienced the rewards of opening up to other women, removing our masks, and endeavoring together to grow from Titus 2 women into Mrs. P-31s. Let us share a few of the rewards we've gained.

Angie's Rewards

As contemporary women, we all fantasize that our children will "arise and call [us] blessed," as the Proverbs 31 lady's did. We love, nurture, and indulge our kids while striving to give them everything life has to offer. We believe that one of our rewards will be grateful, caring, and loving offspring who express gratitude, along with matrimonial partners who regularly praise us for our endeavors. Our fantasies crumble when, instead of our children rising and calling us blessed, with the respect and admiration due us, we are met with the reality of family life:

◆ A baby who rises at 3:00 A.M. to cry, "Feed me."
◆ A toddler who rises out of his bed and climbs into yours at 4:00 A.M.
◆ A grade-schooler who rises to whine, "I won't eat that!" after you have slaved for hours over a hot stove.
◆ A teenager who *never* wants to rise from his bed,

let alone speak to you in the pleasant, respectful manner you so richly deserve.

◆ A husband who, after his hard day at work, will only rise from the sofa if the television remote is out of arm's reach—and you or the kids aren't in the room to retrieve it.

During these times when you feel overworked and under-appreciated, you must remember that God is developing patience, endurance, and fortitude in you. As I rub my knees, callused from nightly prayer marathons, I remind myself that I will eventually experience the rewards Mrs. P-31 experienced.

You must have faith that at the end of your life's journey, you will gaze upon your family while receiving the rich reward of God commending you as a good and faithful servant. Standing at the gates of His great city, if at no other time, your family will, indeed, rise with love and gratitude to call you blessed.

Another reward I have reaped is seeing God provide for the needs of my children who, born with their potentially debilitating disease, are able to live relatively healthy, happy normal lives. I have met wonderful families also dealing with Epidermolysis Bullosa and have been rewarded with some of my greatest friendships. I'm grateful for the women in my small group who gingerly held my emotions and cradled my hurts while showing me faith—faith that God is always there for me no matter the circumstances of my life.

My children, my husband, and I have received the kindness of strangers and friends, and we've been able to travel to places we otherwise wouldn't have. We have also grown more compassionate toward others and their needs. All this because we've learned to trust that God would turn a painful situation into a rewarding and fulfilling one.

Being able to display faith through trials is definitely a reward of being Mrs. P-31!

Pam's Rewards

How do I feel when I read Proverbs 31? Challenged! Mrs. P-31's life dares me to examine my relationship with God and with others. The P-31 woman gives me direction as I read how practically she lived out the priorities of her life. Her maturity, experience, and close walk with the Lord are evident not only in her speech and actions, but also in her attitude.

One of the qualities of the Proverbs 31 woman that I have tried to emulate is her organization and planning. Reading about her accomplishments can easily overwhelm and exhaust you! I believe there were seasons in Mrs. P-31's life where she accomplished many of these tasks, but not necessarily all in one day. They were *lifetime* achievements. Even so, to accomplish what she did in one day or even a lifetime, Mrs. P-31 needed goals, direction, and strong organizational skills.

Verse 16 tells us that Mrs. P-31 "considers a field and buys it." This indicates that she planned ahead. I can envision Mrs. P-31 writing her "to do" list daily and having a calendar close by. No doubt the P-31 woman was also good at setting goals and following through on them. Otherwise she wouldn't have been so productive.

Another reason Mrs. P-31 was able to accomplish so much was she had her priorities in line. Verse 30 indicates the P-31 woman had a close, reverent relationship with the Lord, probably spending daily time with Him. Committing her schedule to the Lord in prayer helped her know what He wanted her to do.

It's so tempting to cut out daily time with the Lord when the "to do" list is long, but that's just when it's most needed. It's amazing how everything falls into place when you're "in sync" with the Lord. Inner joy and peace come from beginning your day with Him.

Another reward of being in sync with God is having children who love and desire to serve Him. I will never forget when my son, Brandon, was nine years old and shared the gospel with his friend, Eric, in the back seat of our car. I could hardly contain myself when Eric prayed along with Brandon to receive Christ as his personal Savior. With tears in my eyes, it was hard to keep my attention on the road!

What joy there is in seeing my children take a stand for Christ. For the past four years, Brandon and Amber have unashamedly led the annual "See You at the Pole" prayer event at their school with other students, parents, and teachers present.

From the Proverbs 31 woman, I have learned that excellence is a lifelong process. It's not so much about being perfect, but about having a Christlike attitude. We need to remember that this kind of attitude starts in our hearts, which determine our thoughts, words, and actions. If our hearts are aligned with God's heart, then we are definitely becoming more like this "excellent woman."

Tammy's Rewards

Proverbs 31:25 tells us that the Mrs. P-31 is "clothed with strength and dignity; she can laugh at the days to come." The *days to come* are so uncertain. Another version of the Bible says that she "smiles at the future" (NASB). What a rewarding and powerful way to live! Is this possible in times like these?

I believe the answer is *yes!* As I look at the personal rewards I have received from living the Christian life for these past twenty-seven years (minus some time off for poor behavior), I would say that rejoicing is at the top of the list.

It hasn't always been so. In fact, by nature I am quite a worrier. I wish I could say that most of my qualms have been about noble things, such as the poor and needy of the world or even the concerns of those close to me. Sadly, most of my ruminating has been about my own life. I'm embarrassed to admit that my sleepless nights have been consumed with thoughts of "What will happen to *me?*" and "What will *they* think of *me?*" However, as the years march on, I sense that God is healing me of my self-centeredness and self-pity. My load is getting lighter, and laughter is literally an integral part of each day.

In the Introduction, I mentioned the great depression — not the economic crash of 1929, but the collapse that occurred in my own life in 1989. Part of what led up to that despair was my overwhelming fear and my drivenness to meet what I perceived to be the expectations of those around me.

I feared for my marriage because my husband wasn't *always* able to make me happy and I frequently disappointed him. I fretted about my children. Was I the kind of mother they needed or would my less-than-textbook parenting cause them irreparable damage? I was fearful about my decision to set my career aside for a season as I focused on my family.

My worries also included relatively trivial matters. Was my house, including the décor and furnishings, meeting the high standard that a few of my friends maintained? And what about my appearance? Could I ever be thin enough or pretty enough? My own health was not nearly as great a concern as slimming down to that ideal dress size, even if it meant insane dieting that ultimately zapped my vitality and joy.

Today I can say that God has turned my sorrow into

rejoicing. This has happened bit by bit over the course of several years. In regard to my marriage, He has shown me that I was too demanding with my husband, expecting him to meet all my needs. I also put pressure on myself to be the perfect wife. After twenty years of marriage, I have learned a simple yet profound truth: *God is the only one who can fill all our longings, and placing anyone or anything else in that role amounts to idolatry.* As wonderful as marriage is, to see it as the answer to all our desires is like trying to fill the Grand Canyon with teaspoons of sand. The exhaustion and frustration would never end.

Joy and freedom come in accepting one another's imperfections and offering grace and forgiveness for pain. I'm so thankful that I've learned to let Jesus be my best friend. Thus, I allow my husband the freedom to focus on things besides me, like his work, our children, and his own spiritual journey. There have been times when we have both wondered if our marriage would survive. Only by God's grace have we kept it together for twenty years, and we trust that as we remain in Him we'll continue on.

The monster of career worry was another battleground for me. My greatest fear in this arena was losing significance. I wondered if I would ever be able to answer with dignity that dreaded dinner party query, "And what to you do?" My concerns were also related to how I would spend my days when I was in my later years and my role as a mother had faded. For years, I tried to keep a foot in several different career doors, from frantically striving to keep my radiography license current to launching a moderately successful small business. It was only after a few sore toes from slamming doors that I became still enough to discover God's plan for my vocation, which has led me to a career in ministry. I still can't offer an impressive answer for that dinner-party question, because when I describe my job directing the small-groups ministry at my church, people are often puzzled. I laugh at the irony that it's simpler to respond, "I'm a homemaker."

What about those "more trivial issues" that I mentioned—my compulsion to make sure that everything external looks just as it should be, including my children, my house, and my figure? It would be dishonest to say that those issues don't *concern* me. The difference is that they no longer *consume* me.

To laugh at the days to come . . . I hope so! I won't accomplish this through the power of positive thinking or through hours spent with self-help books that claim to nurture my inner spirit. Joy will flow in abundance as I am able to forget about myself and focus on loving God and His people. I know the future is bound to hold sorrow. The world is an uncertain place. But I've seen God bring happiness into so many situations that I believe laughter is possible even in the midst of tears, as I stay closely connected with Jesus. This is my reward.

Sandy's Rewards

Like many other women, I used to believe that the description of Mrs. P-31 was an ideal, an unattainable goal. She seemed so perfect. However, just because the passage speaks of her virtues doesn't mean she never had failures, flubs, or foibles. With God's help, we can all become the Mrs. P-31 He wants us to be!

As we learn to follow Titus's instructions with the support of other women in our lives, we gradually develop confidence, wisdom, discernment, strength, nobility, and industry—qualities exhibited by Mrs. P-31. She is a woman of many talents who uses them in serving her family and others. She doesn't obsess about her looks; she's not riddled with guilt; she's not absorbed with her innermost thoughts. She doesn't need to "find" herself, because she's not "lost." She has the assurance that God loves her, that she's special, that she's fulfilling the roles to which she's been called.

The important part of the description of Mrs. P-31 isn't the *tasks* she accomplishes, but the character she develops. And her rewards? She receives praise from her husband and children, and she delights in the accomplishments of lasting value.

As I have tried to live out the qualities listed in Titus 2 and aimed to become like the Proverbs 31 lady, I've reaped many rewards. My marriage is one. It's not perfect, because neither Steve nor I are; yet it is strong, vibrant, and resilient. Our marriage is a testimony that God's plan for marriage does work. Some couples feel like they're living with a total stranger once their children leave home. Steve and I woke up to find we were still friends and lovers with greater freedom and appreciation for one another. We continue to dream, laugh, plan, and work together.

Our children are another reward. Throughout their growing-up years they expressed their appreciation for me in countless little ways. In second grade, Jeff listed me as number one on his list entitled "My Girlfriends." I have long since been replaced—and rightly so—but that list is a special keepsake.

As a preteen, Kristin one day arrived from school to share a revelation she had: "If you took the teaching job at the high school, we would have lots more money!" I explained how our family dynamics would change. She thought a moment, hugged me, and remarked on her way to her room, "I would rather have you here when I come home."

Now both Kristin and Jeff are married. With the love of a mother and the knowledge and experience of a mentor, I have had the privilege to share with them and their mates the things Steve and I learned from our marriage.

Sometimes they've been amazed how similar our conflicts were to theirs. Jeff and his wife, Mandy, have written that our marriage "is an inspiration and example for us to emulate." What wonderful words when they come from those who know you best. Kristin and her husband, Dave, now feel the responsibility and privilege of parenthood. They have peers with whom to discuss parenting and books, magazines, and information galore. So what a reward to have them ask Steve and me for advice, insight, and ideas concerning marriage and parenting.

On those days when your husband becomes angry with you and your children tell you other mothers are much nicer than you, take a deep breath and lift a silent prayer of thanks for the family God has given you. You might not be high on their lists today, but tomorrow they just might "arise and call [you] blessed."

Janet's Rewards

Mrs. P-31 through the years has met many challenges, developed numerous talents, and rejoiced over victories large and small. Her faith has grown as she has tested God's faithfulness one step at a time. She may now sit back for a time and savor the rewards of her earthly efforts. Then again, maybe not!

Perhaps this woman now faces a new challenge — caring for an aged loved one. This is the situation many women of the baby boomer generation experience today. Our children may still be at home or perhaps they have left the nest and have blessed us with grandchildren. Now we are called to assume the role of mother to our aging parents or in-laws.

As I write my part of this final chapter, I am sitting in the oncology ward of a local hospital. My mother has terminal cancer and is coming to the end of her time here on earth. She is going to her reward, her place in heaven! The place Jesus is preparing for her. Talking with her about that great eternal reward and ushering her to those heavenly gates almost makes me jealous that she will then know what heaven is like and I can only wonder for now. If our parent does not know salvation is in Jesus, we may have the joy of introducing them to Him at this time.

My reward now is the ability to do the things she needs done to keep her comfortable and pain free. Is this a reward? Yes, it is! This is a time to discover a whole new way of relating to a parent and learning things about them and our family that we might never have known.

Many of the lessons and trials we have come through in raising our families now become important in caring for the elderly. As they become ill or unable to care for themselves, they may require patience, time, and care to see them through their final days. The many talents and gifts developed will come into practice once again in caring for our parents.

- ◆ *She brings "food from afar."* Remember all those days when you coaxed and cajoled your child to eat what was good for him or her? Guess what? Now those skills will be of use as you entice the aging one to eat nutritious food.
- ◆ *"Her lamp does not go out at night."* All those nights spent sitting at a sick child's bedside where you learned to sleep sitting up will once again be a useful talent as you comfort a sleepless or restless parent.
- ◆ *She "extends her hands to the needy."* Now the needy will be our parents, who will need help with the housework and shopping.
- ◆ *"She is clothed with strength and dignity."* It might require an inordinate amount of strength and

patience to see them through their time of pain and loneliness, especially if they experience an extended illness.

◆ *"She watches over the affairs of her household."* Then comes the time to use those talents learned in caring for the business matters at home and in the workplace. The paperwork of insurance claims and hospital bills will sometimes boggle your mind, but in becoming the women God intended us to be, we have gained insight in how to work through these things.

The closing of this discourse on Mrs. P-31 says, "A woman who fears the LORD is to be praised. Give her the reward she has earned, and let her works bring her praise at the city gate" (verses 30-13). The earthly rewards for each of us will vary because God wired each of us differently. It is, therefore, highly unlikely that one person would possess all of these qualities. So it is good to remind ourselves that the description of the Proverbs 31 woman is a beacon to guide us as we pursue spiritual growth and maturity.

Our Challenge

Even though many women today see the Titus 2 woman and the Proverbs 31 lady as examples of suppression, our desire is that you see the other side of the coin — freedom in following in Jesus' footsteps. Our hope is that you have seen through this study the many possibilities open to you in your desires, ambitions, and spiritual pursuits. While some may have seen serving Christ as a life of suppression, we trust you now see the enormous potential for you as a woman of God.

When life is running like a well-oiled machine (and

occasionally, it does!), realize that you are reaping the rewards of sustaining through the hard times and perhaps emerging from a tough teaching session from God. There is always rain before a rainbow, so don't be surprised when hard work and suffering appear during the journey to becoming a Proverbs 31 lady.

Do you think Mrs. P-31 became "worth far more than rubies" overnight? Just as with diamonds, we might spend what feels like thousands of years under extreme pressure before we are released and seen as something beautiful.

So take heart, women! With God's Spirit residing within you and a mentor, teacher, or friend alongside you, the future looks incredibly hopeful as you continue to grow in Him. We challenge you to offer yourself freely to the world as a much-loved and cherished servant of God, wearing the sparkling and well-deserved crown of life. Well done, good and faithful servant.

DIGGING DEEPER

1. Are the Titus 2 woman and the Proverbs 31 lady realistic models of life for you in today's society? What makes their way of life so difficult?

2. List the rewards promised in Proverbs 31:10-31.

3. What is your definition of the phrase "a woman who fears the LORD" (verse 30)?

4. Do you think as a Proverbs 31 woman you might be limited in your accomplishments due to your roles as mother and wife? Why, or why not?

5. With which subject from Titus 2:4-5 do you most often struggle? What verses from Proverbs 31:10-31 might encourage you in this area?

6. Would your children "arise and call [you] blessed"? Why, or why not?

7. What specific steps might you take to be more successful in your family relationships?

8. Using the letters below, make an acrostic list of the rewards in your life as you grow from a Titus 2 woman into a Proverbs 31 lady.

R

E

W

A

R

D

9. What legacy do you most want to leave in the following areas?
   your marriage

   your work

   your children

   your community

10. Why is a mentor important as you strive to be a Proverbs 31 woman today?

HOW TO FIND A MENTOR

I f you wish to pursue a mentoring relationship, here are important areas to consider.

Traits to Look for When Choosing a Mentor
- ◆ compatibility
- ◆ godliness
- ◆ trustworthiness
- ◆ generosity
- ◆ compassion
- ◆ confidence builder
- ◆ encourager
- ◆ tactful confrontational skills
- ◆ healthy family relationships
- ◆ ongoing Christian growth

Mentoring Cautions
- ◆ Don't let the relationship become consuming or crowd out other important relationships.
- ◆ Don't become emotionally dependent on one another.

◆ Don't put your mentor on a pedestal.
◆ Don't lose your own identity.
◆ Don't let the relationship become exhausting by placing unrealistic demands on one another's time.

Where to Find a Mentor
◆ church
◆ Bible study or small group
◆ neighborhood
◆ classroom
◆ workplace
◆ gym
◆ children's play group
◆ community groups/organizations
◆ volunteer activities
◆ support groups
◆ family/extended family
◆ friend's parent

Examples of Healthy Mentoring Relationships
◆ Ruth and Naomi (book of Ruth)
◆ Mary and Elizabeth (Luke 1)
◆ Paul and Timothy (1 and 2 Timothy)
◆ Jesus and disciples (books of Luke and Mark)

Benefits of Being Mentored
◆ Provides a godly, Christian example to follow.
◆ Encourages spiritual and personal growth.
◆ Creates potential for discovery of your personal gifts.
◆ Builds confidence.
◆ Nurtures a sense of belonging.

ADDITIONAL RESOURCES

Books, Bible Studies, and More

MENTORING

Becoming a Woman of Influence *by Carol Kent*
Between Women of God *by Donna Otto*
The Gentle Art of Mentoring *by Donna Otto*
In the Company of Women *by Brenda Hunter*
Renewal Through Mentoring *by Judy Cagle*

MARRIAGE RELATIONSHIPS

The Five Love Languages *by Gary Chapman*
How Do I Say I Love You? *by Judson Swihart*
The Language of Love *by Gary Smalley and John Trent*
Love Life *by Dr. Ed Wheat*
Loving Your Husband *by Cynthia Heald (Bible study)*
Marriage Builder *by Larry Crabb*
Men Are Like Waffles, Women Are Like Spaghetti *by Bill and Pam Farrel*
Sacred Marriage *by Gary Thomas*

PARENTING

Bringing Up Kids Without Tearing Them Down: How to Raise Confident, Successful Children *by Kevin Leman*

A Family of Values *by John Rosemond*

She's Gonna Blow! *by Julie Ann Barnhill*

See also, the Focus on the Family web site: www.fotf.org

SELF-CONTROL ISSUES

Angels *by Billy Graham*

Becoming a Woman of Freedom *by Cynthia Heald*

The Cry of the Soul *by Dr. Dan B. Allender*

Tame Your Fears *by Carol Kent*

Temptations Women Face *by Mary Ellen Ashcroft*

Tired of Trying to Measure Up *by Jeff VanVonderen*

Who's In Control? *by Karen Lee-Thorp (Bible study)*

Why Beauty Matters *by Karen Lee-Thorp*

PURITY

Becoming a Woman of Excellence *by Cynthia Heald*

The Character of a Christian, *Design for Discipleship Series, NavPress, Book 4*

HOMEMAKING

Celebrate Home *by Angie Peters*

How Not to Be a Messie: The Ultimate Guide for the Neatness-Challenged *by Sandra Felton*

Quiet Moments for Working Women *by Mary Whelchel*

Survival for Busy Women *by Emilie Barnes*

KINDNESS

Dare to Care Like Jesus *by Leslie B. Flynn*
Friends and Friendship *by Jerry and Mary White*
The Friendship Factor *by Alan Loy McGinnis*
I'm Out to Change My World *by Ann Kiemel*
Open Heart, Open Home *by Karen Burton Mains*
Out of the Saltshaker and Into the World *by Rebecca Manley Pippert*
Secret Choices *by Ed Wheat*
Stories for the Heart *by Alice Gray*

SUBMISSION AND AUTHORITY

Liberated Through Submission *by P. B. Wilson*
Me? Obey Him? *by Elizabeth Rice Handford*
Rocking the Roles *by Robert Lewis*

Outreach Ministries

SIDEWALK SUNDAY SCHOOL

Contact: Jan Medvesky at 309-446-3555
Write: Operation Breakthrough
Sidewalk Sunday School
P.O. Box 3701
Peoria, IL 61612
E-mail: janm@gbam.net

CHILD EVANGELISM FELLOWSHIP, INC. (5-DAY CLUBS)

Phone: 636-456-4321 or 1-800-300-4033
Web site: www.cefonline.com

SEE YOU AT THE POLE

Web site: www.syatp.com

CHRISTMAS GATHERINGS (EVANGELISTIC)

Contact: Joyce Bademan at 952-469-4793
Web site: *www.christmasgatherings*.org

CHRISTIAN WOMEN'S CLUBS—STONECROFT MINISTRIES

Web site: www.gospelcom.net/stonecroft/connections

NOTES

CHAPTER ONE: Stepping Back in Time

1. As described by C. W. Cowles, *A Woman's Place* (Kansas City, Mo.: Beacon Hill Press, 1993), p. 98.

2. Joachim Jeremias, as quoted by Cowles, p. 49.

3. Rabbi Judah, as quoted by Cowles, p. 50.

4. Gary W. Demarest, *The Communicator's Commentary Series*, vol. 9, *1,2 Thessalonians, 1,2 Timothy, Titus* (Waco, Tex.: Word, 1984), p. 314.

5. Demarest, p. 315.

6. John R. W. Stott, *The Message of 1 Timothy and Titus: The Life of the Local Church* (Leicester, England: InterVarsity, 1996), p. 189.

CHAPTER THREE: A Heritage from the Lord

1. Margery Williams, *The Velveteen Rabbit* (New York: Scholastic, 1990), p. 9.

2. www.biblestudytools.net, Matthew Henry Complete Commentary on the Whole Bible.

3. Quoted in Steve and Annie Chapman, *Gifts Your Kids Can't Break* (Minneapolis, Minn.: Bethany House, 1991), p. 35.

4. Larry Christenson, as quoted in Jack Hayford, ed., *Spirit Filled Life Bible* (Nashville, Tenn.: Nelson, 1991), p. 901.

5. Dr. James Dobson, "Not Just on Sundays," *Focus on the Family Bulletin*, December 1993, p. 1; quoted by permission.

6. Dr. James Dobson, "Two Basic Kids," *Focus on the Family Bulletin*, January 1991, p. 1.

7. Joel Cox, "Success," *Christian Science Monitor*, February 1979, p. 15.

8. Angela C. M. (Cox) Fortner, "Together," November 1996.

CHAPTER FIVE: **Pure as the Driven Snow**

1. June 1. Sprigg, *Simple Gifts: A Memoir of a Shaker Village* (New York: Knopf, 1998), p. 5.

2. Jack Hayford, ed., *Spirit Filled Life Bible* (NKJV) (Nashville, Tenn.: Nelson, 1991), p. 1930.

3. Susan Hunt, *Spiritual Mothering* (Wheaton, Ill.: Crossway Books, 1992), p. 64.

4. Jerry Bridges, *The Pursuit of Holiness* (Colorado Springs, Colo.: NavPress, 1990), p. 157.

5. Oswald Chambers, *My Utmost for His Highest* (Westwood, N.J.: Barbour and Company, 1963), p. 284.

6. Bridges, p. 157.

CHAPTER SIX: **More than Chores**

1. Dave Barry, as quoted by Paula Jhung, *How to Avoid Housework* (New York: Fireside, 1995), p. 29.

2. Ruth Schwartz Cowen, as cited by Deborah Shaw Lewis, *Motherhood Stress* (Dallas, Tex.: Word, 1989), p. 64.

3. Susan McCarthy, as quoted by Kathy Barberich, *The Fresno Bee,* January 1, 2000, www.fresnobee.com.

4. John R. W. Stott, *The Message of 1 Timothy and Titus: The Life of the Local Church* (Leicester, England: InterVarsity, 1996), p. 189.

5. John Rosemond, as quoted by Paula Jhung, p. 33.

CHAPTER SEVEN: Deliberate Acts of Kindness

1. *www.tvturnoff.org* [August 26, 2001].

2. From *www.preachingtoday.com* [August 26, 2001]. Dorothy C. Bass, quoted in "Reflections," *Christianity Today,* June 19, 2000.

3. Leslie B. Flynn, *Dare to Care Like Jesus* (Wheaton, Ill.: Victor, 1982), p. 39, emphasis added.

4. From *www.sermonillustrations.com* [August 25, 2001]. "Bits and Pieces," December 1989, p. 2.

5. Jerry and Mary White, *Friends and Friendship: The Secrets of Drawing Closer* (Colorado Springs, Colo.: NavPress, 1982), p. 24.

6. Dr. Ed Wheat, *Secret Choices* (Grand Rapids, Mich.: Zondervan, 1989), p. 16.

7. www.christianitytoday.com. Tricia Goyer, "Love in Action," *Christian Parenting Today,* Nov/Dec 1999.

8. Goyer.

9. Quoted by Peggy Anderson, *Great Quotes from Great Leaders* (Lombard, Ill.: Celebrating Excellence Publishing, 1990), p. 31.

10. *www.preachingtoday.com,* as reported by Glen Zander, Portland, OR.

11. From *www.preachingtoday.com* [August 26, 2001].
    Heather Sherwin, "Ordinary Heroes," *Christian Reader*.

CHAPTER EIGHT: **Submit, Who Me?**

1. *Family Ministry,* workbook for "A Weekend to Remember"conference (Little Rock, Ark.: Campus Crusade for Christ International, 1987), p. 102.

2. For more information, see Elisabeth Elliot, *Let Me Be a Woman* (Wheaton, Ill.: Tyndale, 1976), p. 127.

3. Laura Doyle, *The Surrendered Wife* (New York: Simon & Schuster, 2000), p. 19.

ABOUT THE
AUTHORS

Angie Conrad lives in Peoria, Illinois, with her husband, Bruce, and two sons, Andy and Sam. With her many years of experience in leadership, along with speaking at seminars and retreats, Angie encourages others to discover their uniqueness in Jesus Christ. Angie can be contacted at *YAZ001@aol.com.*

Janet Cox is a lifelong resident of Peoria, Illinois, and has been married thirty-five years to her husband, Allen. After raising three sons and a daughter, Janet returned to college and earned her degree from Bradley University. Janet currently serves at her church as a facilitator in a ministry emphasizing recovery. Janet can be reached at Ajaxjack@aol.com.

Tammy Eagan lives in Stamford, England, with her husband, Tom, and their three teenagers. A former radiographer, she currently serves as associate minister of small groups at St. George's Church. You can reach Tammy at smallgroups@stgeorgeschurch.net.

Sandy Kershaw lives in Peoria, Illinois, with Steve, her husband of thirty-three years. The parents of two grown children, Sandy and Steve teach a spiritual growth class at their church and speak together and individually at banquets, retreats, and seminars. Sandy can be reached at skershaw@mac.com.

Pam Miller lives in East Peoria, Illinois, with her husband, Kevin, and their children, Brandon and Amber. Formerly a staff member with The Navigators, Pam now works full-time in a junior-high special education class. She also is a frequent speaker at evangelistic events. Pam can be reached at pammiller87@insightbb.com.

FOUR MORE EXCELLENT TITLES FOR WOMEN.

My Soul's Journey

Perfect for women who wish to journal but don't know how to begin, *My Soul's Journey* uses thought-provoking questions and inspiring topic ideas to help you discover who God wants you to be.
(Carol Kent and Karen Lee-Thorp)

Secret Longings of the Heart

A rich encounter with the hidden desires of women today—the passions that determine lifestyle, behavior, and attitudes—and how these relate to the way you love and serve God.
(Carol Kent)

Detours, Tow Trucks, and Angels in Disguise

Sometimes God is found where you least expect Him to be. Filled with true-to-life stories, this book will make you laugh and cry as you see God at work in your life.
(Carol Kent)

Mothers Have Angel Wings

This special collection of stories about motherhood will inspire, encourage, and challenge you as it explores specific biblical truths and how they relate to being a mom.
(Carol Kent)

To get your copies, visit your local bookstore, call 1-800-366-7788, or log on to www.navpress.com. Ask for a FREE catalog of NavPress products. Offer #BPA.